Walking the Gree

Christian Ucke
Dieter Graf

Náxos and the Small Cyclades

Náxos
Donoússa
Iráklia
Koufoníssia
Schinoússa

**Hiking and Swimming for
Island-Hoppers
30 walks
GPS data**

Graf Editions

How to use this book

The approximate **total length** of the walks is indicated in hours in the introduction to each hiking-route. Time for bus trips or very long rests have not been taken into consideration. Behind prominent spots along the way, **time by foot** is noted at intervals from the starting point.

The **sketches of pathways** have been drawn according to the best of our knowledge, but we cannot take responsibility for their correctness, as they are exposed to continual change since new paths are always being constructed.

For those with a **GPS** device, indications are given in degrees, minutes and seconds. For a rough orientation of distances, the following equivalents may be useful: In north-south direction 1' = 1850m, 1'' = 31 m, in east-west direction 1' = 1500 m, 1'' = 25 m.

Route photos are for your orientation, for asking the locals for information and also to help select your goal. They can be found from ① to ④ in the text. Additional up-dated information can be found under the internet sites on page 144.

The Authors

Christian Ucke is a physicist and has already published a book of walks on Náxos and old travel descriptions of Náxos. He first went to the island at the beginning of the 1970s and is one of the top experts concerning Náxos. He lives in Munich and on Náxos, where he has many friends who supply him with a lot of information about the island.

Dieter Graf is an architect and has travelled all over the world. He also took his first trip through the Cyclades in the years when tourism was just beginning there. Since then he has been attracted again and again to walks in the Aegean. The series of books "Walking the Greek Islands" has originated from these. One of his favourite islands is Náxos.

Contents

Tips for Walking *6*

Climate, Fauna,
Flora,Geology *9*

Mythology,
Historical Data *16*

Phrase book
Explanation of symbols *140*

Náxos

When you sail into the harbour, you can already sense the island's tremendous cultural diversity. To the left, the enormous portal of a classical temple rises up; to the right, you sail past a small Byzantine chapel, and, above the huddled Cycladic city, a Venetian kástro from the Middle Ages thrones. The city, dating back 5000 years, is one of the oldest inhabited places in the world. When you proceed further inwards on the island, the diverse fertile landscapes take you by surprise. An enormous rugged mountain massif forms the background for the green heart of the island, the Tragéa plains, covered with olive groves and ancient oaks. Further westwards, there is wide farming land which winds up in an endless landscape of dunes along the sea. Connoisseurs of small bays for swimming can find wonderful spots along the rocky east coast.

However, not just nature surprises with its enormous abundance. People have also left outstanding constructions during their long history on the island. Except in the industrious Mediterranean harbour city, they lived in small mountain villages which allow us, even today, to trace the tracks of old Greece. In addition to the white-washed cube houses, there are also a great number of castle-like residences from the nobility of the Middle Ages as well as fortress-like Orthodox and even Catholic cloisters. Art-lovers find not only the remains of classical temple complexes but also monumental statues worked on by artists and left behind in the ancient quarry. In the Byzantine chapels from a later period, there are early Middle Age frescoes. Many pieces from the numerous excavations on Náxos can be admired in the local museums.

For many people, Náxos is the most beautiful island of the Cyclades. The pleasantly relaxed manner of tourism will remain in the memory for a long while. Even the gods of the Greek Pantheon felt extremely comfortable here.

Walking on Náxos

"You must traverse it all over to find out the fine parts of it", the Jesuit Pitton de Tournefort noted concerning Náxos in his book "Journey to the Levant" in 1717. Just about 300 years later, this is still true: in order to get to know the largest of all the Cyclades, you must wander around on foot. This book will help you find the loveliest of the old mule tracks. They lead to all the interesting places on the island. There are descriptions from the books "Walking Tours on Naxos" (1984, 1988) by Christian Ucke and "Walking the Aegean Islands: Cyclades" (1999, 2000), by Dieter Graf. Additional newly-found paths have been added. For those who can only visit Náxos briefly, the authors **recommend** walking tours ⑫, ⑬, ㉓ and especially ⑯.

Walking here is wonderful in almost any **season**. Anyone wanting to give his eyes a treat should plan his tour around Easter. It might possibly be somewhat cool and even muddy, but the island is grass-green, poppy-red and broom-yellow, the houses and alleyways are freshly white-washed. Even just the preparations for the Greek Easter celebration are worth the trip. However, you can't go swimming yet, and some hotels and tavernas are still closed.

In May and June, the blossoms are partially withered, but since it is very warm and there are still not many tourists around, this is probably the best time for walking. From the end of May on, the water also has a pleasant temperature.

The main tourist season in July and August is not highly recommended for walking tours due to the heat. The north wind, which blows consistently, still makes the temperatures bearable, but at noon a shady spot under a tree is advisable.

From the beginning of September on, the heat is over and the sea still has a pleasant temperature for swimming until the end of October. Now longer walking tours can be taken again. The land has become brown, the fields bear their fruit, and everywhere you meet friendly farmers harvesting their crops. Starting at the beginning of October, the restaurants and hotels gradually shut down, and some owners travel to their winter residences in Athens. Usually there is a change in climate, with rain in November. Then it becomes unpleasant. For people who want to flee the winter, there is a secret tip: a kind of pre-spring with very warm days occurs in February.

The ancient Greeks used to say, "Nothing is more consistent than change". This is still true today with the old mule tracks, the

monopátia, which have actually become superfluous. Nowadays the farmers prefer the newly constructed streets and roads. For this reason you should always ask about the "monopáti" if you have orientation problems, otherwise you will be directed to roads for vehicles. These, however, are by far not as inviting as the ancient stone-paved monopátia which the farmers trampled along with their mules for centuries. The old tracks are described in this book whenever possible.

Some of what you see in the landscape while walking doesn't correspond exactly to our system of order or environmental responsibility. The Greeks are consistent with their garbage: they are very liberal with it.

The routes described have been walked along again shortly before publication and can be followed by people in normal **physical condition** without difficulty, special firmness of foot is not necessary. Sometimes they are even suitable for children. For longer walking tours, **short-cuts** are indicated. Due to the comparatively thick vegetation on Náxos, finding the way is somewhat more difficult than on the other Cyclades. If you want to walk alone, you should leave information in your hotel. A few **tips** for wandering: mule dung on the paths is more certain to lead you further than goat droppings since the goat paths usually end somewhere in the scrub, while mules always return to their stalls. Steel mesh used as grazing fences can best be climbed over with the help of a pile of stones or at a spot where the "barbs" on top can be turned down most easily. Pasture fences are knotted shut on the side where there are two perpendicular rods. You owe it to the farmers whose land you walk across to shut the openings again afterwards, of course.

No responsibility can be taken for accidents along the walking routes suggested or for possible civil law demands by landowners. Nor can a guarantee be given for bus schedules or opening times. At the end of the book there are **up-dated addresses** which can inform you concerning changes along walking routes and similar new information.

Coloured dots and arrows can often be seen as **markings along paths**, but they do not necessarily correspond to the descriptions in this book.

Red-white metal signs with numbers are new and have been put up by domestic organisations.

A good **map of the island**, from the German publishing house Harms 1:50 000, can be bought on Náxos. There are also good road maps from freytag&bernd and the Greek Road-Editions. The usual Greek maps sold are not suitable for walking tours.

Almost all the starting and finishing points are served by public **buses**, even in the low season. At the bus station in the harbour there is a bus schedule. The departure times from Náxos are adhered to very accurately, but the return times from the villages are less reliable. A few isolated walks away from the larger villages can only be reached by car.

In this case and if no bus is available in the low season, **taxis** can be taken. You should absolutely settle the price before you begin the trip. The taximeter is only turned on when you specifically request it. The high price is considered a surcharge for the poor stretches of road. You can arrange a spot with the driver where you will be picked up later or phone for a taxi along the way. This usually works out well. Another possibility for circular walking tours is a relatively reasonable rental car or a rental motor bike. In addition, domestic car drivers also enjoy taking along a wanderer who waves him down.

Due to the good views, the tours usually lead from the mountains to the sea – so take your swimming gear along.

Sufficient **wandering gear** includes a backpack for a day, shoes with good soles (no sandals), long trousers (or zipper-trousers for the macchia), a mobile phone possibly (in Greek kinitó, a mobile), binoculars, a whistle, picnic equipment and, in the spring and fall, rain gear. A compass would also be good but is not necessary if you have a somewhat good sense of orientation. A GPS device can also be a good help.

Perhaps you should pack Euro electrical adapters and ear plugs (nightly cock-crows!) for your hotel room!

> At this time, the authors would like to express their thanks to everyone who has contributed information for this book.

Climate

Náxos has a typical temperate Mediterranean climate, but with a few peculiarities. In the summer, the average **air temperature** on Náxos is 25°C and thus a bit lower than on the surrounding islands or the mainland. In the winter, the average temperature of 12.4°C is somewhat above that of the neighbouring areas. Náxos thus has a more uniform climate than the surrounding islands. There is frost at sea-level only about one day every fifteen years. The rare snow falling near the sea melts again immediately. In the mountains, however, the snow stays; snow-drifts can even make the main road between Apírantos and Komiakí impassable. The **water temperature** is lowest in February, with 14.9°C, and almost subtropical in August with 24°C.

On a year's average Náxos has about 70 **rainy days** and a precipitation rate of around 400 mm per year (Munich 960, London 600), concentrated in the winter. A total of barely more than 10 mm falls between June and September. The humidity is about 70% throughout the entire year, with heavy dew at night sometimes. The mountainous northern section of Náxos is rather damp for Cycladic conditions, even in the summer. The mountain peaks are often enveloped in clouds from the north.

The sun shines on Náxos on a yearly average of about 2,500 hours (London 1,500; Munich 1,700).

Strong north winds are characteristic of the Cyclades, with three to four Beaufort on a yearly average for Náxos. In the transition seasons, especially in April/May and in October/November, the **Boréas**, a cool, damp north wind, dominates. In the summer, mainly in July and August, the famous etesien winds, called Meltémia (from the Turkish word "meltem") often blow for days. The **Meltémi** blows during the day under a cloudless blue sky, regularly strong from north to northeast, often days on end with velocities of five to six Beaufort. The air is then somewhat overcast and long-distance vision limited. Towards evening the Meltémi slackens somewhat.

The **Schirókko** occurs less often. It comes in hot from the blazing Sahara desert, picks up moisture over the Mediterranean and then reaches the Cyclades, bringing warm humidity from the south.

Fauna

Larger wild animals are not present on Náxos due to the primarily small-sized vegetation. While it is true that stags have been mentioned in earlier travel descriptions, these are probably merely legends.

Goose-vultures ① can often be seen circling majestically, usually in groups, above the peaks of the higher mountains. There are not many now. It is reported that even eagles stop at Náxos every once in a while, and it is certain that there are falcons. A great number of migrating birds fly by the island in the spring and fall. The Greeks are passionate hunters and shoot enthusiastically at partridges, rabbits and other animals during the hunting season.

The wanderer often comes upon the small common lizard, which can be up to 10 cm long. The dragon-like agama (hardun) ② its bigger relative which is up to 30 cm long, is much shyer and attracts attention with its extraordinary posturing, a jerking movement of its head.

The careful wanderer will rarely see snakes. There is only one poisonous type on Náxos: the horn- or sand viper (Vipera ammodytes meridionalis) ③. It can be up to 50 cm long and as thick as two thumbs. A healthy adult hardly need fear a deadly bite.

No death from a snakebite has ever been known on Náxos.

The non-poisonous sand-boa is about the same size; it lives in very concealed spots. The non-poisonous four-striped-adder reaches an adult length of more than a metre and a width almost as thick as an arm. Its size is frightening, but it is harmless, as is its much smaller relative, the ring-snake.

Scorpions, reaching a size of up to 5 cm, also live on Náxos. A bite by this cute little member of the spider family is rather painful but in no case deadly. You can discover crabs, frogs and eels along the rivers which carry water all year round in the northern part of the island. With some luck, you will have the opportunity to see some of the very shy turtles along trail 26. They probably owe their survival to their due to the fact that they are inedible.

You will meet goats and sheep most frequently along the walks. About 40,000 of each are characteristic in the landscape on Náxos. They are shy for the most part and run away frightened when surprised. Even if you can't see them, you can often hear their bells tinkling. The damage caused by their gnawing is quite a problem. There are no more wild goats, as on Mílos.

Flora

In comparison to almost all the other Cyclades islands, Náxos is fertile and rich in water. It was probably covered with forests in earlier times, but little of that exists today.

On slopes and mountain-tops, dry, often thorny shrubs reaching a height of up to half a metre predominate, often in the form of hedgehog-shaped cushions (phrígana in Greek). Broom ①, thorny knap-weed (centauria spinosa), heather, spurge plants and poterium spinosa are some typical representatives.

Thicker bush or tree groups with evergreens up to double man-size and bushes with hard leaves (macchia, in Greek xerovumi) are not found as frequently. Juniper and mastic bushes are particularly predominant.

In protected, water-rich valleys and plains and near the course of rivers, there are higher trees such as the kermes oak and stone oak. The flora is, on the one hand, characterised by the climate. Precipitation amounting to about 400 mm in the winter and a hot summer with a dry period of almost six months favourise xeromorphous plants, i.e. plants which have efficient mechanisms for economising or storing water and preventing evaporation: small leaves, needles or thorns, leaves or stems which are coated with wax or else fleshy. The strong Aegean winds – the etesian winds – impair vegetation and often cause bizarre, crippled growth of bushes and small trees on open slopes. There are obvious differences in plant growth between the damp, mountainous northern section, where clouds dispense rain with the north winds, and the flat, dry southern section of Náxos, with its smaller forests, individual trees, eagle fern and scrub.

Mankind has also influenced floral life on the island quite drastically. Through deforestation with ensuing erosion, former great tree reserves have been lost irreversibly. By turning mountain slopes into pastures for voracious goats, even the beginnings of more vegetation have been checked. In addition, through incidental or intentional fires, ground erosion is increased further. The wanderer often comes upon such burned areas with coal-black stumps. The purpose of planned fires is partially to open up new freshly growing green areas to feed the goats. In the short run, this goal is possibly achieved, but inedible plants grow just as quickly, for example phlomis fruticosa, asphodel ② or sea-onion. The long-term effects are thus very disputed.

The terraced fields with expensive irrigation systems are characteristic on the steep slopes and give witness to the island's fertility. Their cultivation is toilsome, and their partial deterioration helps erosion even further. For several years now, increased cultivation of vines on new terraces can be observed. Is this perhaps a compensation? About 400 ha of land on Náxos are used for wine-growing, mainly in the north near Apírantos, Kóronos and Komiakí.

In order to protect the agriculture from the strong winds, a reed called arundo donax, which grows several meters high and is often confused with bamboo, has been planted. All the drift sand plains on the west coast of Náxos (Livádi, Engarés, Pláka), which are used intensively for agriculture, form true labyrinths with this giant reed. Although it offers the wanderer welcome shade, it can nevertheless cause orientation difficulties. The reed is also used for various forms of basketry. It was formerly used in house-building to make or support diverse wall and roof constructions. It is still often seen as an awning or sunshade.

A main product cultivated on the fields is the seed potato. The quality of the Naxian seed potato is famous even beyond Greece, and it is widely exported, while cooking potatoes are less common. In addition, barely, wheat, tomatoes, cucumbers, artichokes, pumpkins, melons, etc. are cultivated. Greenhouses for intensive cultivation are also on the increase. Agriculture on Náxos has only local importance since the land has been split up into relatively small plots.

The cultivated plant leaving the most conspicuous imprint on the countryside is without doubt the olive tree ③. In the central part of the island, the Tragéa plateau, it forms entire forests. Altogether there are about 400,000 olive trees on about 900 ha of the island. Grain is still often cultivated on the ground protected by the olive trees.

There are smaller groves of evergreen oaks in the Tragéa, Mélanes, Sangrí, but few fir or pine-tree forests. Near the coast, especially on beaches, there are tamarisks and Mediterranean junipers which are non-demanding and can tolerate the salt. Plane-trees shade the village squares and also exist numerously outside the settled areas, along riverbanks. High, slender cypresses traditionally decorate cemeteries. Occasionally palms can be seen in old gardens, a remnant from the Venetian period. Acacias, araucarias, poplars, alders, maples and eucalyptus trees can also be found.

In the spring, almond trees bloom, especially in the area around Potamiá. Plantations with oranges, lemons and varieties of the orange family are found in Engarés, Mélanes and Sangrí. The Naxian liqueur speciality "kitron" comes from the leaves of these trees. Apples, pomegranates, pears, plums, apricots, cherries and figs grow here. Mulberry trees exist on Náxos as a result of the silkworm farming that used to take place here.

Agaves (agave americana) often line the streets, lanes and paths. This thorny leaf plant has only grown in the Mediterranean area since the 16th century. Fig-cactus is also wide-spread.

A surprisingly abundant splendour of flowers appears in the

spring. Even in January there are anemones and crocus blossoms. From February to April the flowers are in full bloom: rockroses, iris, daffodils, hyacinths, cyclamens, lupines. Blossoming broom bushes add a lot of yellow to the landscape. The bright red of the poppy stands out in the meadows and along fields and paths. Golden-yellow chrysanthemums in the background increase the impression.

The orchids are an adornment of spring, if only for a short time. Their small blossoms can easily be overlooked, but they develop every exotically. Over 30 different types have been found on Náxos. Ophrys, orchis, and serapias can be seen more frequently. ④ ⑤

From February to June the asphodel (asphodelus) ② blooms. This plant, which grows to a height of more than a metre, is not eaten by livestock, not even by goats. The withered stalks last all year.

In May and June the main blossoming season comes to an end. The dull red or white blooming marigold South Africa only opens around noon. Summer doesn't mean brown desert, by any means. In protected spots blossoming plants can still be found, especially the red-blooming oleander bushes ⑥. True thickets of oleanders are spread along the river-courses even in summer and point out where dampness is present.

In the late summer and fall, the flora begins to come alive again

after the first brief rain showers. Meadow-saffron, heather and sea-onion reveal themselves along with the crocus-like stellaria bergia, dandelions, thistles and cyclamen.

Many sorts of plants in the Phrígana, the macchia, contain ethereal oils. In the heat of the day you can appreciate especially clearly the pleasantly spicy aroma of thyme, rosemary, lavender, oregano, camomile, fennel and sage since the effect of these substances becomes more powerful in the warmth. If you step on a thyme bush, entire aromatic clouds cover the area. If you rub the leaves between your fingers, you can enjoy a broad palette of familiar smells.

Geography and Geology

Náxos, with an area measuring almost 430 km², is the largest island in the Cyclades Archipelago. A mountainous massif, the highest elevation in the Cyclades with its main peak Zeus 1,000 m high, crosses through the island from south-west to north-east. The relatively young mountain-forming powers in the Mediterranean region still keep the outer zone on the Cyclades in the south (Mílos, Santoríni, Anáfi), from the Golf of Corinth to the coast of Asia Minor in movement. Earthquakes are frequent in those areas, but not on Náxos.

In the east, the geological structure of Náxos consists of a metamorphic complex whose core is formed from a dome made of magmatic gneiss, cut into horizontally by erosion. This is an area rich in water extending from Potamiá to the Kóronos mountains. Around this core there is an alternation of marble, slate and amphibolites (transformed magmatic stones).

The frequent alternation of slate – marble is also clearly recognisable in the landscape: darker, greenish zones of slate bear more bush vegetation since they are richer in water. They are permeated with bright yellowish-pink bands of marble which are almost free of vegetation and can hardly retain dampness due to the porosity of their dry chalk formation.

The entire low western part of the island, from the city of Náxos to the sandy beaches in the south, is made up of a young tertiary granodioric massif which submerges under the present sea level towards the west in the direction of Páros. Characteristic weather-worn forms are the numerous blocks, some of which have been hollowed out, and the final outcome being coarse sand.

Naxiotic **marble**, known since ancient times, doesn't have the excellent quality found on Páros. Traces of old quarries can be found around Mélanes, near the Kúros, Sangrí and Apóllon. Nowadays the main mining area lies south of Kinídaros, where entire rounded mountain tops have been carried away. Smaller quarries process marble into gravel for building houses and streets. Most of the marble is exported, and only part of it is processed here. The workshops are on the outskirts of the city of Náxos, on the road to Chalkí and near Kinídaros. They can be visited. Marble is a soft stone which has long been valued among sculptors for its good workability. Lime, which is used to white-wash the houses on the Clyclades, is extracted from marble.

Emery from Náxos has been known since ancient times. It is a very hard, heavy mixture of magnetic iron ore, mica and corundum and has been used for polishing since early times. It is found bedded in marble and has been mined, sometimes according to mining standards, in the region between Apírantos, Kóronos, Liónas and Mutsúna. It can be recognised by its rust-brown colour. There is a museum in Kóronos to document the history of emery mining on Náxos and also a visitors' mine. In addition, there is also a small geological museum in Apírantos (ΓΕΟ–ΛΟΓΙΚΟ ΜΟΥΣΕΙΟ ΣΜΥΡΙΔΙΣ, Pétru Protopapadáki).

Mythology

Many myths are connected with Náxos. Zeus, Apóllon, Diónysos, Démeter and Ariádne are the most important deities who were worshipped here and whose cult was significant. The classical figures still live on today in the names of castles, villages, streets and hotels.

Diónysos (Roman: Bacchus), the god of wine and ecstasy, was, without any doubt, the main deity of Náxos. For a while it carried his name directly as Dionýsia. The powerful, uncompleted statue in the quarry near Apóllona is attributed to him, and a temple dedicated to him was discovered in 1986, south of the city Náxos.

Diónysos gave the island the gift of the grape vine. Grape-bearing Náxos is a saying, and the island's wine is celebrated in songs as the prime of all Greek wines. In ancient times there was even talk of a marvellous wine spring. In ancient representations on coins or vases Diónysos can often be seen with all his symbols: kántharos (drinking cup with two handles), crater (bowl in which wine was mixed), thyrsos (staff wreathed in ivy with grapes), grapes.

It is doubtful that Diónysos was born on Náxos, but a cave near Engarés is called Jénnissis, which means birth-cave. Diónysos was brought up by the nymphs Phília, Korónis and Kleíde, according to one local legend in the cave Kakó Spíleo. The name Korónis still lives on in the mountain-range and village bearing her name.

There are many sagas about Diónysos, the most famous of which is probably how Diónysos saved **Ariádne** on Náxos after she had been abandoned there by the unfaithful **Theseus**, who had killed the Minotaur, Ariádne's half-brother in the labyrinth on Crete.

While fleeing from Crete to Athens, he went ashore on Náxos and left Ariádne asleep on the islet of Paláti, situated before Náxos. Even today, near the present Hotel Apóllon, there is a place which is called in Ariádne's Bath or Spring.

Only the gods know why Theseus willingly left her there for Diónysos – in any case, the god married Ariádne. The god of wine was handsome and had brought along sweet wine. Ariádne quickly forgot Theseus` perfidy. Ever since, the wine from Náxos has been considered a good remedy for offended love. One Naxian legend maintains that the two spent their first night of love in the Cave of Zeus, a place which doesn't seem very inviting for this purpose. Ariádne's bridal wreath was placed in the heavens as the constellation Coróna Boreális. The northern crown in the sky. Ariádne herself became an immortal deity.

Zeus (Roman: Jupiter), the father of the gods, is said to have spent his youth on Náxos. It seems doubtful, however, that the cave bearing his name and located on the side of Mount Zás or Zévs was really his birthplace. A more plausible version relates that he was born on Crete and raised on Náxos by an eagle. From this bird of prey he received the bolts of lightening which he used so vigorously. Zeus left Náxos to fight against the Titans. During the ascent to the peak of Mount Zás you pass by the very old inscription 'ΟΡΟΣ ΔΙΟΣ ΜΗΛΩΣΙΟΥ' (Mountain of Zeus, Protector of the Herds) engraved in a marble block. Coins from Náxos with a picture of Zeus on them testify to his local veneration.

The numerous legendary love-affairs of Zeus had a variety of consequences for Náxos. He begat with his sister Démeter – the goddess of the earth and of fertility – a daughter, Persephone. A reconstructed temple near Sangrí is dedicated to Démeter. Léto bore him Apollón. He seduced Seméle, the mortal mother of Diónysos and later appeared to her in his divine form, causing her to burn to ashes. Zeus himself then carried the six-month-old embryo to term in his hip.

In legends Náxos is connected with Thrace and Caria. **King Boréas**, whose name is given to the summery north storm, reigned in Thrace. His son Butes was banned along with his companions because of conspiracy. He came to Náxos, and, as a pirate, made the world unsafe from there. He called the island Strongyle (the Round One).

He allegedly seized Iphimedeia and Pankratia, mother and sister of the Aloiades Otos and Ephialtes, on one of his plundering raids and brought them to Náxos. The giant Heroes quickly set out to free their close relatives. Their sister died during the struggle, and afterwards they stayed on the island, which they called Dia (the Divine). Because of their arrogant blasphemy, **Artemis** had a hind run between them during a hunt. Each of them wanted to kill it with his javelin, but they struck and killed each another instead. On Náxos people say that both of the uncompleted Kúri lying in the quarries of Flério near Melanes represent the island's Heroes, Otos and Ephialtes.

During another assault, Butes raped the beautiful Korónis, a follower of Diónysos. As punishment he was struck insane and drowned himself. The Thracians finally left Náxos because of a period of drought.

The deserted island was later resettled by Carians under their leader Náxos, who gave the island its name.

Even **Apóllon** played an important role on Náxos. The temple directly before the city is attributed to him and indicates that the Apóllon cult was cultivated on the island. Near the village of Apóllon in the north of the island, the inscription ΟΡΟΣ ΧΩΡΙΟΥ ΙΕΡΟΥ ΑΠΟΛΛΩΝΟΣ (Border of Apóllon's Holy Region) can be seen near the Kúros which probably represents Diónysos. Apollo was also worshipped on Náxos as the Shepherd God. In the Classical Period there were numerous Naxiotic foundations for the famous places of worship to Apóllon on Delos and Delphi.

Historical Data

The island of Náxos experienced two historically brilliant periods: the Archaic Period in the 7th and 6th centuries B.C. and the Venetian Epoch in the 13th and 14th centuries A.D. Important architectural structures or the remains of temples and castles from both of these epochs are still preserved.

Náxos was relatively unimportant in the other time periods and thus remained untouched by many difficulties. Nevertheless, the island's relative wealth in comparison to its neighbours' continued to attract pirates and intruders.

Neolithic Period (5000–3200 B.C.) First traces of Stone Age settlements on the Cyclades are found on the island of Saliágos near Páros. The first inhabitants of Náxos were possibly Thracians. Later the Carians came from Asia Minor.

Cycladic Culture (3200–1100 B.C.) In the Bronze Age Europe experiences its first artistic zenith in the **Early Cycladic Period** around 3200–2000 B.C.

The so-called Grótta-Pélos culture with highly developed ceramics and the famous marble idols comes into existence on Náxos. Many of these can be admired in the museum in Náxos. Trade connections exist with other islands and the mainland. The Keros-Syros culture blooms around 2400 B.C., with fortified settlements on Náxos (Kórphari ton Amígdalon near Pánormos) and Keros, one of the Small Cyclades. In a burying-place in the southeast of Náxos, oil lamps and pitchers have been found, the first reliable indications of the cultivation of olive trees and wine-growing.

In the Middle Cycladic Period around 2000–1600 B.C., Cretan settlements arise on Náxos under Cretan-Minoan influence.

In the Late Cycladic Period from 1600–1100 B.C., after the decline of the Cretan-Minoan culture (around 1450 B.C.), Mycenaean influences increase, as proven by excavations near Aplómata (City of Náxos).

Geometric Epoch (1100–700 B.C.) In 735 B.C. the Ionians come to the central Cyclades. Due to over-population, another Náxos is founded as the first Greek colony on Sicily. For this reason, Náxos is also called "Little Sicily". A cemetery near Tsikkalarió produces findings from this period.

Archaic Period (700–490 B.C.) In the 7th and 6th centuries B.C., Náxos shows its dominance over Delos with the magnificent avenue of the lions. Marble work reaches a peak; the Kúri, the statues of youths, are made and the temple of Diónysos is constructed on the Livádi plain. In 538 B.C. the Ionian Lygdamis gains power over Náxos and reigns as a tyrant. Under his rule the temple of Apollón is begun but never completed. Náxos probably has about 100,000 inhabitants. In the battles after his fall from power in 499 B.C. the Persians attack for the first time.

Classical Period (490–336 B.C.) In 490 the Persians Datis and Artaphernes land on Náxos, destroying the city and its shrines and enslaving the inhabitants.

The brilliant period on Náxos is ended. The island must serve the Persians militarily but does so with resistance. The ships Náxos contributes cross over to the other Greeks even before the Battle of Salamis in 480 B.C. In the 5th and 4th centuries B.C., Náxos joins both Attic sea alliances. Due to efforts to become independent from Athenian domination, Náxos is besieged by the Athenian fleet in 466 B.C. and forfeits its independence.

Hellenistic Epoch   (336–146 B.C.) Náxos passes under the power of Macedonia, Egypt, Rhodes and finally Rome.

Roman Epoch   (146 B.C.–330 A.D.) In 146 B.C. the Cyclades become a Roman province with Délos as their trading centre.

Byzantine Period   (330–1207 A.D.) In the 4th to 7th centuries Christianity spreads. The frescoes in the Panagía Drosianí are from this period. There are attacks by Vandals, Slavs and Saracens.
In the 8th and 9th centuries the new Islamic ideas also influence Greece. In a feud over pictures, iconoclasm, the admissibility of a pictorial representation of God and the Saints is disputed. Some wall paintings from this epoch, often referred to as the "dark period", still exist in churches on Náxos, for example, birds and fish in Agía Kiriakí near Apírantos (walking tour 22).

Venetian Epoch   (1207–1566) In 1204, under the order of Venice, the Crusaders conquer Constantinople during the 4th Crusade.
Following this, in 1207, Marco Sanudo, a nephew of the old Venetian doge Dandolo, establishes a Roman Catholic duchy on Náxos. Páros, Sífnos, Mílos, Ios, Santoríni and Anáfi belong to his domain. In the 13th century the Sanudi enlarge the fortress in the city of Náxos, build the castle Apáno Kástro in the interior of the island and construct the Catholic cathedral. After this time, there is a Catholic archbishop on Náxos. The island Iráklia in the Small Cyclades is also fortified by a castle.
In 1344 the Turkish corsair Anur attacks Náxos and carries off thousands of women and children to be sold as slaves.
After 1383 the Venetian Crispi dynasty rules. The defensive battles against the Turks increase. The Turkish sultan's dreaded admiral, Chaireddin Barbarossa, lands on Náxos in 1537; the island must pay tribute and comes under the influence of the Ottoman Empire along with the other Cyclades.
In 1566 the last duke of Náxos, Giacomo Crispo, is deposed and dies in Venice.

Turkish (Ottoman) Epoch   (1566–1821) In 1566 Sultan Selim II invests his Jewish governor, Joseph Nasi, with Náxos. Jewish refugees settle in the town district Evraikí in Náxos. After 1579 Náxos comes under direct Ottoman rule but is ruled loosely from Constantinople, retaining relative independence. For this reason, many churches and most of the pírgi are built during this time. In 1651 the Venetians win a sea battle against the Turks in the straits between Náxos and Páros, but there is no renewal of their reign over Náxos or the other islands.

In the 17ᵗʰ and 18ᵗʰ centuries pirates plunder the Cyclades despite Turkish sovereignty. Thus the Small Cyclades are deserted by their inhabitants for centuries, and the islands serve the pirates as a hide-out. During the Russo-Turkish war from 1770–1774, the Russian admiral Orlow sails to Páros and Náxos with his fleet and gains certain trade and sea rights for the Cyclades. Jesuits, Ursulines, Capuchins and Lazarists come to Náxos and found monasteries and schools. In 1787 construction of the orthodox cathedral is finished.

Independent Greece (since 1821) On Náxos itself there are no conflicts during the war for independence against the Turks. The Naxians contribute to the fight for freedom elsewhere. The Catholic aristocracy on the island does not fight on the Greek side during the struggle for independence, of course causing itself considerable difficulties later.

The Small Cyclades are once again populated by the cloister Amorgós, but they have still retained the name "Nisídes", "Deserted Islands".

In 1833 the Bavarian-Greek King Otto I visits Náxos. Travellers and engineers from Western Europe came to the islands more frequently after its independence. The great Cretan poet Níkos Kazantzákis visits the Franciscan School in Náxos from 1897 to 1898. After 1898 the harbour is enlarged.

Twentieth Century During the inner-Greek differences between the supporters of the King and those of the Prime Minister Venizelos, Apírantos is fired upon by a warship in 1916. After 1922 Greek refugees from Asia Minor come to Náxos after the defeat against Turkey and settle in the town district of Paraporti. In the Second World War first the Italians, from 1941 to 1943, then the Germans occupy the island. The Kástro is bombarded by the British at the end of 1944; shortly after, the island is handed over by the Germans.

The Greek Civil War from 1945 to 1948 results in no conflicts on the island, but opposing political views remain among the inhabitants.

In 1973 the Catholic school affiliated with the Ursuline cloister in Kástro is closed after 300 years.

After 1980 tourism begins to have a strong influence on the economical and population structures. The airport is constructed in 1992, reservoirs are built with funds from the European Union. In the same way, the system of roads and the power supply, which comes from Páros, are developed further. A new section of the city with numerous hotels arises between the old city of Náxos and Geórgios Bay. The drachma, the oldest currency in Europe, is replaced by the euro in 2001.

❶ Island Panorama

A long circular walking tour of approximately
4 hours/8 km from the city of Náxos. The first, easier
part leads to a – non-accessible – monastery with
a fantastic panoramic view. This tour is also a nice
sunset walk in the evening.
During the second part of the route, several fences
must be crossed, so you should be familiar with paths.
The difference in altitude of about 300 m is not
that strenuous. On this route there are no tavernas.

Start at the monument at the **Náxos** harbour (GPS N 37° 06' 26.5
E 25° 22' 28.2'').

> *The statue represents P. Protopapadákis from Náxos, who, a*
> *minister of state, was implicated in the defeat in the war against*
> *Turkey in 1922, the "Asia Minor disaster", and then shot.*

Proceed towards the northern coast along the path closest to the
coast (dirt road parallel to the asphalt street to Engarés) past the
former – archaeological excavation sites Grótta and Aplómata.
Still in the city, close to the Orthodox cathedral, there is a new
museum which is worth visiting, exhibiting remains of excavations of Náxos' significant early period.

After passing the Hotel Grotta, you might be lucky enough to
see – among a lot of new buildings – the small chapel **Agía
Paraskeví**, also called Ágios Fanúrios (¹/₄ hr/N 37° 06' 35.0"
E 25° 22' 56.0''). Ágios Fanúrios is considered to be the saint to
call upon in order to recover lost things. Past the chapel, go down
the steep steps to the asphalt road leading to Engarés and follow
this road about 200 m to the northeast.

At this point, a road turns to the right; the sign (ΜΟΝΑΣΤΗΡΙ ΑΓ
ΧΡΥΣΟΣΤΟΜΟΥ; Saint Chrysostom) shows you the way to the
monastery. The road ascends in serpentine curves and can easily
be shortened by taking the trampled footpaths, heading directly up to the monastery. Halfway there, to the left, there is a picturesque little chapel named **Ágios Ioánnis Theológos**, built into the rock. Then you reach the cloister.

> *The orthodox **Chrysóstomos Monastery** ① (also page 144)*
> *(³/₄ hr/N 37° 06' 34.0" E 25° 23' 35.0'') was built in 1606*
> *but contains older building elements inside. It presents a type*
> *of fortified Pírgos monastery which is found more than once on*
> *Náxos. This one is still inhabited by a few nuns. Admission of*
> *visitors is hardly possible any more.*

James Theodore Bent, an English traveller and archaeologist, reports descriptively and very vividly about the conditions there in the year 1883:

On Christmas afternoon we walked up the hillside behind Náxos to visit a nunnery dedicated to St. Chrysostomos, into which we were told no males would be admitted without special permission from the bishop. On reaching it we entered a low door without opposition and climbed a ladder which conducted us to a storey of empty cells; it seemed like a charmed palace, this huge empty nunnery, as if inhabited by some spellbound princess. On our descent, however, we came across and terrified three nuns just coming out of their cells, whose surprise may be imagined at seeing two fair-haired males descending a ladder and introducing themselves as "angels", that is to say, Αγγλοι, or Englishmen, on Christmas Day. For some time the ignorant old things were too bewildered to speak, and it was long before we could make them understand who we were, and what our object was in thus intruding.

If you don't arrive at the monastery too late in the day and are not scared off by a stretch of about two to three hours, take the dirt/cement road to the left of the monastery through the gate, cutting off the way. You may have to climb over the fence.

The destination is a white-washed building high up on the ridge to the east. A few metres after the gate a small path which can hardly be recognised turns upwards to the right. Paths like this look quite clear at the beginning but soon vanish into air. These ridge paths are trampled upon by animals, but are also used by people.

Continue up to the pen, whose fence can be opened easily, and then walk along the fence to the left through a gate made of an old bedframe until you reach an agave which can be seen from

the distance. There is water here, and an oleander bush is quite close by. The **ridge** (1¹/₄ hr/N 37° 06' 37.7" E 25° 24' 03.2") with the white-washed building can be reached quite quickly now. From there, you can overlook the interior of the island: to the east you have a view across the fertile Engarés valley lying far below and on across to the Mélanes valley, just as green. You can even see the bare peak of the Kóronos, which is the second highest mountain on Náxos. To the west and to the north you have a magnificent panoramic view of Páros and – in clear weather – you can see many other Cyclades islands, unfolding on the horizon.

Approximately 100 m to the right of the white-washed building to the northeast, you pass an opening in the wall and reach a relatively clear path *between* two fences made of steel mesh and a bedframe gate near a small building. Don't open the gate, but, instead, climb over the wall near the building. Continue northeast until you reach another typical Greek bedframe gate. Pass the other buildings and then continue past a small vineyard on the right. Climb over the fence and proceed to the northeast of the fence. If you pay attention, after a few minutes, you can see the white barrel roof of the almost hidden chapel **Ágios Fokás** ② (1³/₄ hrs/N 37° 06' 27.9" E 25° 24' 41.8") in the northeast. You will find a cistern with water and reeds, clearly indicating dampness. Quite a lot of cactus plants grow in this area.

Pass to the left of the unimposing chapel and continue south to southwest across the fields, crossing all walls or fences that might be there. Further to the south, a broadcasting transmission pole is a good point for orientation. A few hundred metres further, you may possibly stumble onto a path eventually meeting a somewhat wider path, which, however, is hardly recognisable since nowadays it is rarely used. This **path** runs from west to east (2¹/₄ hrs/N 37° 06' 11.0" E 25° 24' 28.2"). If you miss this opportunity because you have gone too far east and reach a dirt/cement road, then continue on this road to the right until you reach a **red point** (N 37° 06' 10.8" E 25° 24' 46.0"), where the mentioned path turns again to the right. Follow the path to the west. It is a lovely and comfortable high route, leading you back to Náxos in an hour. Unfortunately, the path is slowly getting overgrown due to the lack of intensive use, so it will probably not be able to be used anymore in a few years. Along the way, down to the left, you can see the little village of Angídia. In the distance, the fertile Livádi plain with its characteristic protective belts of reeds stretches out. To the right, you have a complete

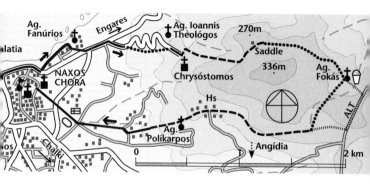

view of the double peak on the Stelída peninsula with Páros stretching out directly behind it.

After a while, you will reach the cement section of the path, which is only about 100 m long. If you continue to the west, the small chapel **Ágios Políkarpos** (3 hrs/N 37° 06' 13.9'' E 25° 23' 37.1'') can be found along the path bordered by agaves and oleander bushes. Further down, you will reach cemented streets, leading to the **Catholic cemetery**, the sports field across from it and a hotel complex in bungalow style, before you finally arrive back in the city of **Náxos**.

➋ To the Stelída Peak

An easy walking tour beginning in the city of Náxos and leading along the beach to the Stelída peak.
A good part of the route can be walked barefoot, but not the way up to the Stelída peak. The entire stretch of about 5 km can be walked in two to three hours, even when accompanied by children. The tour can be completed with a swim at the Ágios Prokópios beach. It is possible to return to Náxos by bus.

Begin at the chapel **Ágios Geórgios** ① (GPS N 37° 06' 05.8'' E 25° 22' 24.2''), after which the beach behind it was named. Along the beach there are various snack-bars and restaurants as well as surfboard and boat rental places. After these, there is an area with wide sand dunes which may be covered in "idyllic" plastic garbage, especially after strong winds. Windsurfers usually train in the bay, particularly in July/August. It is a pleasure to watch the experts surfing at a wind velocity of 5. Náxos is very popular among connoisseurs. Finally, you reach a **dam** running from east to west ($^{1}/_{2}$ hr/N 37° 05' 11.8'' E 25° 21' 38.5''). The dam blocks off an area that is normally filled with water in spring after rainy winters and offers a refuge to many birds. In the summer, the lake is usually dried up; then one can walk or even drive through it. The Náxos airport was constructed here from 1985 until 1992, which has had very negative effects on the island's flora and fauna.

Follow the asphalt road on the dam a short stretch westwards towards the Stelída peak. At the fork in the asphalt road, turn right and leave the road to walk along the bank of the hill. This means a bit of climbing since there is no clear trampled path. Later on, there is a rather steep mount to reach a dirt road rising in serpentine curves directly to the ridge between the two peaks. From here, you can easily reach the higher **peak** ($1^{1}/_{4}$ hrs/37° 05' 11.5'' E 25° 20' 44.9'') on a clearly visible path marked with cairns (piled rocks). The Greek military took away lots of earth and blasted rocks out of the Little Stelída in order to construct the new airport. This is why the area looks quite furrowed now.

> *Alternative:* At the fork in the asphalt road, continue straight ahead until the road turns slightly to the left. Then turn right onto a dirt road leading steeply upwards and continue to the ridge between the two Stelída peaks.

From the **Stelída peak** (150m) you have a wonderful view over Náxos and far beyond. Stretched to the south, there are the wide sandy beaches Agios Prokópios, Agía Anna, Mikrí Vígla, Kastráki, Alikó and even Pirgáki. Right behind the coast at Agios Prokópios, there are three lakes which almost have a mauve colour and from which salt for the olive harvest in autumn is still extracted from time to time. On a clear day, the silhouettes of several of the Cyclades can be recognised on the horizon: to the south Ios, Santorini, Síkinos, Folégandros; to the north Syros and Tínos. To the west, one has a view of the whole of Páros.

From the western side of the Stelída peak it is quite easy to reach

the paths leading to the southern beaches. From the peak you start walking to the west and continue on past the small house of a Swedish painter, almost built into the cliff, until you reach a dirt road leading steeply down to the south. This area is becoming more and more built up with studios and apartments. Almost at the beginning of the Ágios Prokópios beach and directly at the end of the asphalt street, there is a restaurant called "Katarina" (1³/₄ hrs/N 37° 04' 43.2" E 25° 20' 35.0"), where typical Greek food is served under shady awnings. A bit further on, there is the chapel **Ágios Prokópios** (2 hrs/N 37° 04' 42.8" E 25° 20' 29.9"; closed), after which the beach was named. Walk past the salt lakes and behind the dunes until you reach the narrowly built-up settlement Ágios Prokópios.

It is a bit more strenuous to walk barefoot along the lovely, coarsely grained sandy beach. At the end of the wide beach, you reach the asphalt street again (N 37° 04' 24.3" E 25° 21' 07.6"), from where the bus – usually packed with people in the summer – returns to Náxos Chóra. A lot of tavernas along the way invite you to enjoy a meal there.

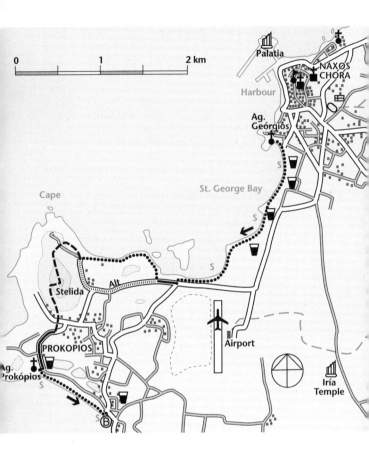

❸ Over Cliffs and Fields

This easy walking tour leads from Ágios Arsénios, through an intensively cultivated agricultural area and on past a bizarre cliff chapel to the dune beach and Agía Ánna. The stretch of approximately five km can be walked comfortably in three to four hours. The tour ends at the beach, where you can go for a swim or have a refreshment.

Take the public bus towards Trípodes/Pirgáki. The bus stops on the road near the school in **Ágios Arsénios** (GPS N 37° 03' 49.8" E 25° 23' 44.1"). To the southwest you can see the ruins of two windmills on the crest of a hill. To the right of these, about 400 m away, Ágios Spirídonos, the imposing main church of the village, can be seen. It shows its three naves, a white dome and two tiled bell towers. A little further behind, but still in the village, there is the church Ágios Nikólaos.

Take the small cement road towards the south and then continue to the southwest through the long village until you reach the church **Ágios Spirídonos** (¼ hr/N 37° 03' 43.5" E 25° 23' 27.7").

> *Ágios Arsénios, also called Agersaní, is a village not yet much affected by tourists. There are some Kafeníons where you can buy something to eat or make other purchases.*

Approximately 50 m after the main church Ágios Spirídonos, follow the village path, cemented at the beginning, to the southwest. Along the way cactus plants, agaves and reeds alternate. The entire area is intensively cultivated. After approximately 400 m, the white-washed chapel **Panagía i Zoodóchos Pigí** (Holy Virgin as Life-Giving Source; open; N 37° 03' 28.0" E 25°

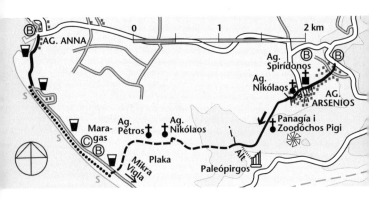

23' 13.7") appears on the left side of the dirt road. The way leading to the south becomes more narrow and slightly ascends.
Once you have reached the **ridge** (1/2 hr/N 37° 3' 21.5" E 25° 23'
5.3") of the chain of hills, which have a height of 40 to 60 m, you
can make out, down to the left, the remains of the tower of the
Paleópirgos, standing alone at a height of approximately 10 m.
Far to the south, there is the jutting cape of Mikrí Vígla with its
wide sandy beaches and dunes.

> *Alternative:* There is no direct way to the Paleópirgos from
> here, but you can go down on small trampled paths. Once
> there, you can hardly see more than from above ④.

Turn towards the west, but ignore the red arrow pointing to the
right near a farmyard. The dirt road goes straight, almost along
the ridge, through a bizarre rocky landscape. Some pastures and
fields are here. On a gate in the middle of the path a sign in Greek
warns "Beware of the dog!" If the gate is open, you can try to continue directly along the dirt road. If not, a path directly in front
of the gate leads down to the left. After a short way, you suddenly
have a view over the west coast of Náxos; in the distance you can
see the peak of the Stelída hill and Páros.
The fertile alluvial land in the foreground is one of the agricultural centres on Náxos; the entire area is called Kalamúria. The
famous seed potatoes of Náxos are grown here. Grain and veg-
etables also flourish in this area since there is sufficient water and
an extensive pipe system for intensive artificial irrigation. Meanwhile, however, so much water is being pumped from the wells
that there is the danger of too much salt near the sea. More and
more cube houses are being constructed here. Since they are only occupied during the two months of the main season, the sub-

division of the farming land may already be characterised as quite dubious.

As you descend along the path, you will discover at the right, somewhat isolated attached to an overhanging rock, the tiny bright white chapel **Ágios Nikólaos** ① (³/₄ hrs/N 37° 03′ 25.5″ E 25° 22′ 36.4″).

Down in the lowlands, in the middle of a field, there is the chapel **Ágios Pétros** ② (1 hr/N 37° 03′ 24.8″ E 25° 22′ 23.5″). A little before it, to the left of the path, you can see the unusual marble sculptures of a resident artist.

In about 20 minutes you can now walk in a zigzag line along lanes lined with reeds to the **beach of Pláka** (1¹/₂ hrs/N 37° 3′ 13.7″ E 25° 22′ 0.5″) and then walk barefoot along the beach to the right to **Agía Ánna** (2¹/₂ hrs/N 37° 04′ 01.8″ E 25° 21′ 21.7″). In the summer, an active beach life reigns here with lots of tavernas and discos to satisfy your physical needs. There are also two big camping sites. On the road parallel to the beach, buses drive to the city of Náxos. **Agía Ánna**, a rather bland place, offers many restaurants and also a bus stop.

❹ To the Dunes of Pláka

*From Vívlos (Trípodes) you go down an attractive,
though somewhat overgrown path (long trousers
recommended) onto a fertile plain and wander on
between the fields to the sand dunes of Pláka.*

In the **ditch** at the southern end of the village of **Vívlos**, below
a large church with several towers, there is a vehicle track which
leads along the edge of the large valley to two chapels. Go to the
right past the first chapel enclosed by a fence. In front of the second, **St. George's Chapel** (¹/₄ hr) ①, turn left beneath the ruins
of a watchtower and then right 60 m further on, onto a path leading to a rural chapel in the valley. Here you make your way to the
right through some reeds, then a few metres uphill until you
come across a secluded path, where you bear right. You soon
come to a **grotto chapel** (¹/₂ hr) between the rocks.

The path continuing on into the valley is now somewhat overgrown and is crossed by a vehicle track. Down in the **plain** (³/₄ hr)
turn left onto the stream bed, and you will find paths covered
with reeds ② and leading to a cement way. If you take this to the
right for several steps, you will come to the ruins of an old tower, the **Paleópirgos**, also called Pírgos Plákas.

> *The remains of these walls made of square hewn stones set to-
> gether without any mortar used to be a Hellenic fortress-tower
> which was encircled by a farmstead.*
>
> *This kind of fortified rural colony was commonly found in the
> Aegean area. In addition to work and living areas, the tower al-*

so offered protection during attacks due to its five to seven stories and its walls about one metre thick. In ⑱ you pass by a better preserved example of this ancient type of construction. James Bent was here in 1883: "Next morning we rode off to an Hellenic tower, called Pláka, which has guarded one of the most fertile little plains in Náxos. About fifty feet of this tower are left standing, and one window; the tower was nearly square, being ten and a half yards by twelve and a half yards, and stands on a gentle eminence, and is built, as usual, of mortarless stones, long and flat. Close to the tower we saw several graves cut in the rock, and about two hundred yards from the tower is a granite quarry, from whence the stones to build the tower were evidently cut."

After this, follow the cement way to the sea. After walking along two cliffs, you will come to dirt roads again. Unfortunately, they do not lead straight to the sea, so it is perhaps better to take a shorter route across a field or to follow the signs to Mikri Vigla and then take the right fork down to the hotel resort on the sea front. One way or another, you will arrive at the endless sand dune beach of **Pláka** (1½ hrs). Here there are tavernas and a bus into town. Sometimes the bus departs only from Maragas campsite (to the north).

It would take 2½ hours walking along the coastline to reach the town of Náxos from here on foot.

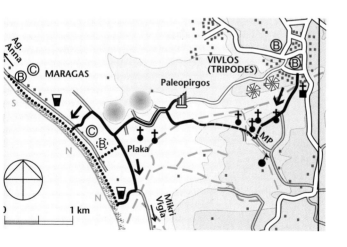

⑤ The Temple of Démeter

A four-hour trek to the partially re-erected Temple of Démeter and on over a plateau with tilled fields to the long, sandy beach of Pláka. There are no tavernas en route; long trousers are an advantage.

Get off the bus at the **Sangrí turn-off** and walk 600 m along the road to the village of **Ano Sangrí**. (Sometimes the bus stops nearer the houses). Turning right ahead of the village, bear left of the monument in the small grove of pines, down onto the concrete road and then left later on along the paved path, to the deserted monastery of **Agios Eleftérios** (¼ hr) ①. Though it is certainly worthwhile going on a few steps to see the small, clustered village!

Opposite the monastery, to the right of a stone gentleman with a bow tie, climb down the steps and wander along a defile in the direction of a chapel up on the hill to the right. Go a short stretch along a worn path and then onto the dirt track below the hill chapel ②. Do not follow the sign to the Temple of Nikólaos, but head straight on along the dirt track. On the left, you see a wide plain with olive trees and, opposite at an angle, the temple ③ on a hill. When the dirt track ends above a shed, follow a red arrow to the right, later climbing down left (arrow) into a hollow. At first go right without a trail for a short stretch, and then left at the monopáti, to the middle of the valley through the dry bed. You arrive at the **temple** along hidden paths (¾ hr).

The Temple of Démeter dates from the 6th century B.C. It was used for diverse purposes and rebuilt several times during the course of history. It was nevertheless possible to ascertain its original form and reconstruct a certain part of it. See page 40.

Now return along the original path and, directly behind the temple, join onto a roadway into the valley, past the small museum. Continue without a trail under some olive trees through a hollow, then uphill through the phrígana until you come across the monopáti you used earlier. Turn left here. On the left above is the re-erected temple: one can take pleasure in the fact that an ancient temple has again become part of this delightful landscape which holds a close relationship to the mountains and the wide plain. A site which only the ancient Greeks could have chosen! Next trudge on through a **hollow** (1 hr), which is sometimes wet, take a field track on the right immediately after and then, before the olive grove, make your way up left without a trail to the ridge. Heading along the road at the top in a northerly direction, take a look back towards the temple! The point of departure in Ano Sangrí is visible up on the right. At the **crossing** (1¼ hr, sign in the opposite direction: Dímitras), the way leads straight on ▣. You are surrounded by wide fields and solitary, shady trees, much punished by the wind: ideal resting spots for both humans and animals.

Now take the left fork at the **junction** (1½ hr) leading over the hill which marks the boundary of the plain. The dirt road passes a gravel works (left) on the way down and ends at the **road** (1¾ hr). You have to march energetically 100 m along it to the right, until you are below the chapel on the slope. Opposite (on the left-hand side of the road) is a walled entrance leading down to some fields. Head across country for 120 m until you find a dirt track leading up right from the hollow. Later on, when some walls appear up ahead, turn left along the path and then, shortly after, bear right ahead of the farmhouses.

Enjoy the peaceful path between the rocks which leads to the **slope** (2½ hr) above the sea, where there is a break between the

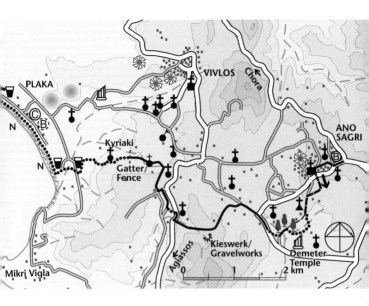

rocks. At first, head down along a track-like path, then, without a trail, over thorny terrain to the Kiriakí chapel at the foot of the slope. Then on from the **chapel** (3 hr), along farm roads lined with reeds, to the **dunes** ahead, where you can tear off your clothes!

To reach the bus into town, it takes another 35–40 minutes via the beach, where you have the opportunity to examine both the architecture of the sand-castles and the stature of their creators. The **bus** leaves from the **campsite**.

Temples on Náxos

Besides Délos and Páros, the only important temples of the Greek Classical Period in the Cyclades can be found on Náxos. Here, three temples have been excavated and examined. German archaeologists played an important role in these excavations.

The **Temple to Apóllon on the Palátia peninsula**, with its mighty portal (page 4), greeting all visitors, has never been completed. The previous construction there had also been dedicated to Apóllon, the god of light. Temples dedicated to Apóllon facing Délos existed on several islands. Every year there was a great festival, and, simultaneously, celebrations took place on the surrounding islands. In clear weather, it was probably possible to see the light signals from the holy island. Around 530 B.C. the tyrant Lýgdamis started building the temple, which is still clearly recognisable today. With exterior measurements of 24 x 55 m and a pillar height of about 13 m, it would have become one of the largest temples of those days. The portal, which is has an unusual depth and was set 1.20 m above the ground, was possibly used as a stage for political purposes or oracles. The actual entrance was located at the side. 1000 years later, the temple was transformed into an early-Christian basilica and another 1000 years later, it was used as a quarry for the Chóra by the Venetians.

The **Temple to Démeter in Sangrí** ⑤ ⑧ was discovered by the Greek archaeologist N. Kontoleon in 1949. He noticed the great number of architectural fragments in the isolated chapel of Saint John. Together with some farmers, he located the first pieces. His later excavation in 1954 and especially the German-Greek excavation between 1976 and 1995 proved the uniqueness of this rural Ionic temple. Its size was 12.6 x 13.2 m, and, except for two wooden doors, it was completely out of marble. No signs of an altar were found. There were two equivalent side entrances from the entrance-hall, the *Pronaos* in the main room and a windowless *Cella*. The roof was covered with marble tiles 2–4 cm thick which allowed the light to shine through from above! The cult chamber also had another special characteristic: walls that had been left in their original rough condition. When the doors were shut, one had the feeling of being in a cave. This leads to the assumption that celebrations to the earth and fertility goddesses Démeter and Kore took place here at night, until the first daylight came through the ceiling of the room. Cavities for sacrificial offerings, hewn into the stone platform in front of the temple, also prove that Démeter was worshipped.

During several reconstruction measures to build the church, the exterior wall of the temple was taken away around 500 A.D., and, in addition to the basilica, a small cloister with an inner courtyard was added.

The tremendous accomplishment of archaeologists and architects consisted in being able to visualise the ancient temple and the early-medieval basilica among approximately 1600 fragments scattered all over, some of which had even been built into the walls of farmhouses. Then the chapel of Saint John was taken apart and moved aside, and the temple was put together as a puzzle with the original marble fragments and the others new. The contour of the basilica is visible again. All these efforts have been supported by funds from the European Union, which are certainly much better invested here than in some of the other measures regarding infrastructure.

The **Temple to Diónysos of Iría**, south of the city (map, p. 30) was discovered by G. Gruben and V. Lambrinudakis in 1986. The approximate site had been known from reports. After intensive questioning of some of the farmers in the potato fields, the right spot could be located. Excavations revealed four levels of temples exactly on top of each other. The most recent, the upper level, had measurements of 13 x 29 m and was in a walled-in sanctuary measuring 100 x 60 m. Nowhere can the development of the Cycladic temples between the 8th and 5th centuries B.C. and of the Diónysos cult be seen better. The excavation field has now been covered again and secured. It may be visited, but very little is recognisable.

❻ On the Southern Cape

*Here the hiker will encounter one of the most
beautiful beaches for swimming on Náxos, but he
should be prepared to exert his strength during
an eight-hour-tour of 22 km. One can also get there
by taxi, rental car or motor bike. The only tavernas
are in Agiassós, and they are only open during
the high season. Good walking shoes and a sufficient
supply of water are of great importance!*

Drive to **Agiassós** (GPS N 36° 58' 5.8" E 25° 25' 27.7"). Walk
along the dirt road about 800 m to the south until you reach a
turn to the left (N 36° 57' 44.6" E 25° 25' 39.9"). Follow this dirt
road approximately one kilometre and then walk along the river bed on paths which are easily recognisable in the beginning,
then continue about 300 m, although there are no further visible paths, and ascend to the **crest** (2 hrs/N 36° 57' 35.3" E 25°
27' 31.7") of the chain of hills in the east.

From the crest you can see, south to southeast, the Erimonísia,
small islands lying to the south of Náxos. Walking tours for these
islands are described at the end of the guide. In good weather,
Amorgós can be recognised behind these islands, Ios is in the south.
In the northeast – fitting into the surroundings very well and
hardly recognisable – there is the Tower of Chimárru ⑯, which
can actually only be seen through binoculars. The next destination along the route – the Bay of Kalandós – is to the southeast.
From the crest, continue towards the southeast (there is no path)
through relatively light undergrowth with man-high bushes,
moving slowly downhill. Further on, you will reach the slopes
heading downwards to the east. Some of these slopes have steep

sections which it would be better to avoid. In this way, you will arrive almost directly at the Bay of Kalandós. By bearing left, you can, however, go down to the dirt road and then to the bay along this road to the south.

The **Bay of Kalandós** ① (4 ¹/₂ hrs/N 36° 56′ 9″ E 25° 28′ 9.3″) has one of the most beautiful beaches on Náxos. Only in the absolute high season (mid-July to mid-August), is it perhaps possible to get food or drink there. At other times the beach is usually deserted since it can only be reached by car via a rather long and poor dirt road. Apparently, there are plans to construct a ho-

tel complex in this area. This will hopefully still take some time. At the western end of the bay, there is the small chapel Agios Theodóros. Walk past this west to southwest on a rather recognisable path. Pass above a piece of property on the coast surrounded by a high wall. You will reach sea level again. Then go up rather steep 70 m. The poles of an old electricity line will help you get your orientation. From above (N 36° 55′ 13.8″ E 25° 27′ 1.2″) you can see the southern cape of Náxos: **Ákra Katoméri** ②, and, further to the south, the island of Iráklia. Ios is behind it, along with further islands.

Pass the bay of Órmos Stivú, where underwater cables to the southern islands begin (6¹/₂ hrs/N 36° 55′ 15.2″ E 25° 26′ 44″; sign ΔEH). There are several caves along the rocky coast. A dirt road leading to Agiassós begins in the next bay. In the bay after it, which opens to the west, there is the quaint little chapel **Ágios Sóstis** ③ (Άγιος Σώστης; 7 hrs/N 36° 55′ 30″ E 25° 26′ 14.7″). Stay on the dirt road for approximately 6 km until you return to Agiassós. You will still encounter some strenuous ascents. In Agiassós there are some tavernas, but, unfortunately, they are usually closed during the low season.

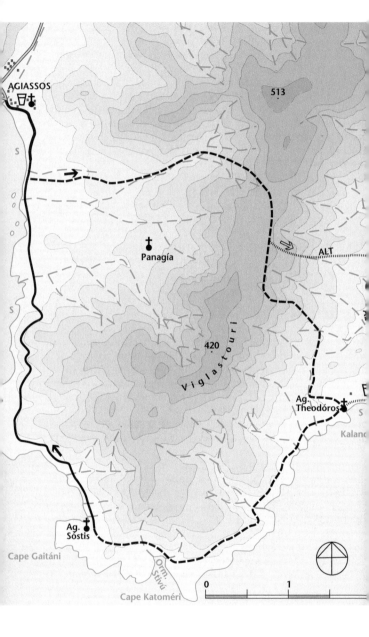

AGIASSOS

513

Panagía

ALT

Viglastouri

420

Ag.
Theodóros

Kalanc

Ag.
Sóstis

Cape Gaitáni

Orm.
Stívú

Cape Katoméri

0   1

❼ Into the Plain of Tragéa

An easy trek to whet your appetite, through the olive groves of the Tragéa plain. Two and a half hours over easily identifiable tracks and paths with a pleasant stop at a taverna in Chalkí.

The most difficult part comes straightaway: explaining to the bus driver that you want to get off at the turning to Agiassós (or Tímios Stavrós). Here you head along the road between the **petrol station** and the windmills, up to the bulky, unadorned **pírgos of Tímios Stavrós** ⑧.

The original 17th century fortress-tower of the Baséou family was later converted into a monastery. A fertile plain, which reaches right down to the sea, spreads out below – watched over by the Temple of Démeter on the hill in the centre.

Directly behind the monastery, a path ascends up to the left over slabs of rock and into the olive groves. You wander along cheerfully: to your left is the wide valley protected by the Venetian castle up on the highest mountain. Then turn right at the fork to the **reservoir** (¹/₄ hr). The dirt track leading past the olive groves is lined with nut bushes ①. In September, preparations are made for the harvest: tightly woven nets are spread beneath the olive trees ②, and the olives are then knocked off. At the next fork, wander straight on to the hollow where you come across an attractive paved stone path through a field. Bear right ahead of the fence, down onto a shady path which later becomes a wide field track. Soon the beautiful plain of Tragéa, which remains green all year, lies ahead. The torso of a windmill is visible up left on a hill; but continue to march on unwaveringly below. The field track makes a left-hand bend – this very spot is the beginning of the

footpath up to the **small church** ($^3/_4$ hr) on the hilltop ③. If you prefer not to take a break here, continue downhill along the track taking in the attractive, green surroundings as you walk. On the right, between some trees, you have a view of the hamlet of Damalás and, above in the distance, you see the mountain village of Moní. When you come to the vehicle bridge alongside a chapel, turn right and, 50 m further on, bear left onto a roadway lined by ancient olive trees. Later, at the junction, take the more attractive way down right into a dry bed, before going up a few steps to **Hímarros** ($1^1/_4$ hr) and the road. Here, the relentless Cycladic wanderers can head uphill past the cemetery, turning right at the small church on top before heading down again, contentedly, over a splendid paved path and on left below.

> *Short cut:* You can continue along the asphalt road and 400 m further on, turn off left between a house and a chapel ④.

Take the unpaved way straight ahead and turn down right into the dry stream bed (blue arrows) immediately after. On the other side there is a sunken way leading into the village.

> ▷ By heading through the olive groves left of the path, you can reach the beautiful church of **Ágios Geórgios o Diasoritis** (George the Rescuer), an attractive example of a Byzantine cruciform domed basilica of the Tragéa. The way is posted on a sign in Chalkí. Open until 2 pm.

Keeping right at the first houses in **Chalkí**, take a look onto the square to see who else is sitting in front of Jannis' taverna. Later on, you can get the bus at the church of Protótronis.

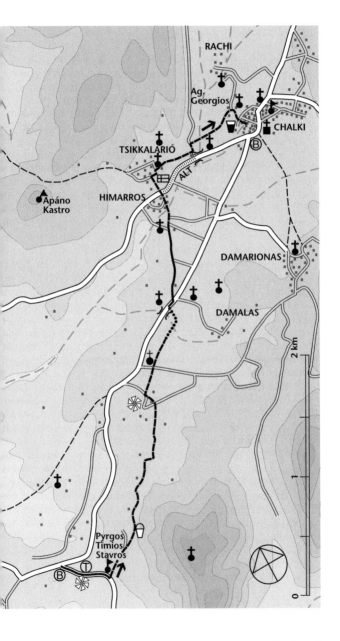

RACHI

Ag.
Georgios

CHALKI

TSIKKALARIÓ

ALT

HIMARROS

Apáno
Kastro

DAMARIONAS

DAMALAS

2 km

1

Pyrgos
Tímios
Stavros

0

⑧ Temple and Cave

On this tour you visit the partially reconstructed Démeter temple and continue on to a church hidden in the rock face and further to a Venetian Pírgos. It takes about three to four hours for this beautiful seven-kilometre circular walk. The temple museum is open daily, except Mondays, from 8 a.m. – 2 p.m. The trip there and return are by bus.

Before you reach the Tragéa plateau, there are three villages lying closely together: Káto Sangrí, Kanakári and **Áno Sangrí**, the southernmost village. The bus stop is situated at the side of the road (GPS N 37° 02′ 33.7″ E 25° 26′ 32.4″). From here, walk westwards on the road to the village, passing a small wood of pine trees on the left and then, at a fork in the road, on to the left through the village. On the southern edge of the village stands a small **obelisk** with a bust of Konstantin Xenákis (¹⁄₄ hr/Κωνστ Ξενάκης; N 37° 02′ 24.9″ E 25° 26′ 06.0″). Opposite lies the abandoned but non-accessible **monastery of Ágios Eleftérios** from the 14ᵗʰ century (see ⑤ ①). Descend south on the narrow path beginning at the bust. On the right above the path there is the chapel of Agía Paraskeví (see ⑤ ②). Far to the east you can recognise the brown-grey Pírgos Tímios Stavrós, at the foot of the mountain Profítis Ilías, which is the end of the walk. The path continues slightly downhill between agaves.

Alternative: Should you wish to see the Byzantine **chapel Ágios Nikólaos** (N 37° 02′ 12.5″ E 25° 26′ 12.3″), turn left after 300 m onto a small path at the signpost. In five minutes you will reach the picturesque chapel which was built around the 12ᵗʰ century and has wonderfully restored frescoes. The chapel is locked, but if you ring the bell someone may perhaps come and let you in for a small contribution. Some way further on is the Byzantine chapel Ágios Ioánnis. In the area around Sangri there are numerous ancient Byzantine churches with precious frescoes. After a short time you will recognise the Diameter temple on a small hill to the Southeast and next to it a small chapel (see ⑤ ③). Above a shed (arrow), continue to the right. A lovely donkey trail runs above a valley planted with olive trees. Later a beaten track marked by an arrow forks left into the valley (¹⁄₂ hr/N 37° 01′ 56.7″ E 25° 25′ 55.1″). This leads through the often wet valley bottom and then once more uphill and directly to the temple n 2001 the entire temple site (³/₄ hr/N 37° 01' 45.1" E 25° 25' 2.0") ①, including a well-endowed museum, was made accessible to the public.

> The beautifully situated classical **Temple to the Goddess Démeter** dates from the 6th century B.C. In about the 5th century A.D. the temple, without any great structural changes, was transformed into an early Christian church. In the 6th century A.D. there was probably a basilica which used only a small part of the temple foundation. This church site was most like-

> ly raided and destroyed by Saracens in the 8th and 9th centuries and looted in the following centuries. The ruins were later used for agricultural purposes. Finally the small chapel Ágios Ioánnis Gírulas was erected over the foundations of the temple, constructed with a large quantity of antique building parts. In 1949 this was noticed by an archaeologist who then started investigations. More about this can be read on page 40.

Continue on towards the northeast through the field and slightly uphill. The quarry, now hardly recognisable, used for the construction of the temple, was located here. Soon, to the northeast, you can see Pírgos Tímios Stavrós, which you will steer towards. At the beginning there are only beaten tracks.

Along the way you pass the inconspicuous natural stone coloured Byzantine **domed church Christós** (1 hr/N 37° 01' 46.7" E 25° 26' 08.1"), which is first hidden behind olive trees. A further chapel is to the right. Direct access is hindered by fences. Now follow the paths leading towards Tímios Stavrós. The landscape is surprisingly varied: from olive groves and fruitful orchards to barren, stony fields.

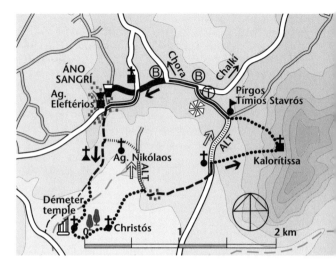

Short cut: About 1500 m after the temple, you can take a dirt track to the left. At a later fork in the track, take the path that turns to the left to come to the **chapel Ágios Nikólaos** (see above). From here you can find the way back to Áno Sangrí.

After a bit more than 2 km, you come to the asphalt road leading from Sangri to Agiassós on the coast.

Short cut: If you go along the road to the left, you will come to Pírgos Tímios Stavrós.

Several ruins can be seen about 100 m uphill on a mountain slope to the northeast. A monastery was once here. Hidden behind it ★ the 13th century **cave church of Kalorítsa**, Kalorítissa (the Bringer of Luck) (2 hr/N 37° 02' 12.4'' E 25° 27' 16.8''). Those who still have energy in reserve may want to attempt the almost direct 100 m-climb to this church, but without a path and taking about 30 minutes. At the top you will be rewarded with the panoramic view over the whole countryside from Sangrí to as far as the city of Náxos. The deserted-looking cave church is locked but through a hole in the rock face you can get a good impression of the site ②. In these kinds of hidden places priests taught children secretly during the Turkish rule.

Afterwards, continue without a path northwest downhill to **Pírgos Tímios Stavrós** (2½ hr/N 37° 02' 23.7'' E 25° 26' 59.0'').

Pírgos Tímios Stavrós, Pírgos Baséu (Τίμιος Σταυρός ο Πύρ-

γος Μπαζάιου; the True Cross) dates from the 17th century. In-
side there is also a small chapel. The Baseos family, from whom
it has its name, purchased it in the 19th century. In 2000 it was
fully renovated and is now open for cultural activities such as
exhibitions or concerts.

From Tímios Stavrós walk down to the main road and turn left
here to the bus stop at Áno Sangrí, which, of course, you already
know.

Early Literature on Journeys to Naxos

In this book we have included descriptions of journeys made
by the following travellers:

James Theodore **BENT** (1852–1897) was an English traveller
and archaeologist who travelled the Aegean in 1883/84. His
book "The Cyclades, or Life among the Insular Greeks", 1885,
is regarded as a classic and was republished in 1966 in its original form.

Ludwig **ROSS** (1806–1859) was a well-known German archaeological researcher. He travelled to Greece in 1832, where
he was appointed Head Curator of Antiquities by King Otto in
1834 and, in his capacity as curator, got to know the country
and its people intensively. His report "Reisen auf den Inseln
des griechischen Meeres" (Travelling the Islands of the Greek
Seas) was published in 1841.

The Frenchman Joseph Pitton de **TOURNEFORT** was a
botanist and also studied theology and medicine. At royal
command he travelled to Greece from 1700 to 1702. His descriptions even have a scientific background. The first French
edition of his famous work "Relation d'un Voyage au Levant"
was published in 1717.

Ernest Aristide **DUGIT** (1834–1900) was a professor of litera-
ture and Ancient Greek in Grenoble. His thesis "De insula Na-
xo" (1867), is one of the most extensive descriptions of Náxos.

➒ Venetian Pírgi

*A four-hour trek through Arcadian landscapes
to Filóti. Walk along the old main path through the
island, protected by ancient tower-houses or pírgi.
These medieval fortress-towers were the easily defen-
sible country residences of the Venetian nobility.
About 30 such towers still exist on Náxos.*

It's best to tell the bus driver where you want to get off shortl
before you get there, i.e. Káto Sangrí. (There is a marble factor
on the left, just before the road turns off to K.S.). The bus stop
at a stone **bus shelter opposite the road to Káto Sangrí**. Fo
low the disappearing bus for 200 m along the road, leaving it a
a right bend and turning onto a field path straight ahead. Ther
is a power line on the left. On the way down, you see the first in
habited pírgos ① against the backdrop of Apáno Kastro, the mai
Venetian fortress in the hinterland of the island ①. In the valle
below lies a large, noble country residence of a newer kind. Cros
the **dry stream bed** (¹/₄ hr), taking the roadway up left to th
★ church on the hill shortly after. Go straight on ahead at the for
and turn off right at the left bend onto the wide, old road pavec
with flat rocks, which used to lead from the Tragéa plateau to th
harbour. From the paved road you can soon see a beautiful, olc
(but regretfully locked) cruciform-domed basilica ② and anoth
er pírgos (Baséou or Tímios Stavrós), in the background. Then
after some ruins on the right-hand side, the track becomes los
in the rock, and you must let yourself be guided by the wall or
the left.
After passing a polygonal building, you come to the **road** (³/₄ hr)
which you cross in the direction of a windmill torso. (There is a

ather tall pasture fence ahead of the windmill, however, which
ou can avoid by going left along the road for a short stretch).
ehind the windmill, head down to a roadway, which you fol-
ow to the right for ten metres before turning off it to the left di-
ectly afterwards.

ou are now on the fertile Tragéa plain with its large olive groves.
ligh walls on the right lead you safely through, past the small
illage of **Damalás** (1 hr) in the hollow, protected by an attrac-
ive domed church. Hike on to the village of **Damariónas** (1¹/₂

ir). Right at the start of the village, at the corner of a house ③,
ead into a maze of alleys, turning right before an archway and
hen down to the **war memorial** on the asphalt road.

> *Alternative:* You can reach **Chalkí** over small mule tracks
> in 15 minutes: take the steps to the left of the memorial,
> first keep to the right and then to the left at the two forks,
> go to the right behind the bridge and then turn left again
> directly afterwards, passing the sports field on your right
> and going through the narrow pass. Then, keeping left
> of the houses, you'll arrive at the washing facilities in
> Chalkí.

he way from Damariónas to Filóti leads up to the right of the
nonument. At the next fork, you bear left and are soon at the
ipper end of the Tragéa plain on a roadway with a great view,
urrounded by olive trees. No matter how hard you try, you will
iot lose your way here and thus have all the time in the world
o look out for more pírgi. Three can be seen at once – two in
Chalkí and one in Keramío.

3elow Filóti, take the bridge over the hollow, then the dirt road
o the right directly after and wander on up, between gardens ④
)eneath Mt. Zás, to the inviting street cafés of **Filóti**. The clever

owners, of course, know exactly when the next bus will arriv
and that there is still time to stop for refreshment under the plan
trees. If you're interested, you will also find a pírgos south of th
main church here in Filóti.

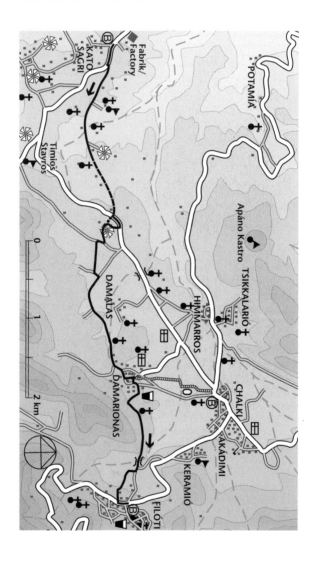

⑩ Kástro Apalíru

Besides the famous Apáno Kástro, Kástro Apalíru is the most important castle on Náxos. It consists practically only of ruins now, but is impressive because of its tremendous size.

If you go by bus, you must walk a rather long stretch along an asphalt road. A rental car or motor bike would be better. The walking tour itself is easy. There are no tavernas.

Take the bus to the bus stop in the village **Áno Sangrí** ⑦ and then follow the main road at first. At the fork in the road, take the road to the right which leads past **Pírgos Tímios Stavrós** ① to Agiassós. About two kilometres after the pírgos, a dirt road turns off to the left. A sign (Κάστρο Απαλίρου; ¹/₂ hr/N 37° 01′ 25.8″ E 25° 26′ 32.3″) marks the turn-off.

Follow this lane about 1.5 km. At the end, the path makes a wide curve to a house with pens (1 hr/N 37° 00′ 57.1″ E 25° 26′ 55.1″); a jacked-up white VW bus is another point of orientation. Nearby there is a sign from which a not very distinct path ascends southwards directly to **Kástro Apalíru**. After about 1¹/₂ hours you reach the remains of the outer wall ② surrounding the entire castle complex, approximately in the middle of the castle's ground-plan (N 37° 0′ 42.9″ E 25° 27′ 9.1″). From above you can imagine why the castle was built here: it offers a dominating view of the entire surroundings.

In *'Byzantine Castles on the Kyklades'* Hannalene Eberhard describes the complex:

> *The colony above the valley of Agiassos was on the slope of a mountain, protected by a large fortress on the summit, Kástro tu Apaliru. This castle was held by the Greeks and the Genuese in the year 1207, and Marco Sanudo could only conquer it after a siege lasting many weeks. It is thus the only fortress from the Middle Ages on the Kyklades proven through historical facts and in writing to exist in the Byzantine period, even before the reign of the Venetians. A report of another event concerning the castle indicates an even earlier time period: in the year 850 Arabs are said to have conquered it, thereby making themselves masters of the island. Unfortunately, there is no confirmation of this through written evidence.*
>
> *The castle complex covers the entire upper area of the mountain, from its northern to southern points in the back through*

the east ridge area of the mountain to deep within in the western slope. Its length is about 350 m, with a width of about 50 m on the northern end and the greatest width of about 90 m on the southern end. The difference in height within the castle area is almost 60 m from east to west, the inclination from north to south is about 30 m.

Authors of older descriptions of Kástro tu Apaliru state that it had three walls surrounding it. Except for a small stretch of wall on the slope which is probably the remainder of the wall surrounding the former small village there, only one wall is actu-

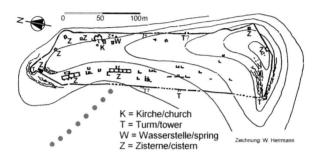

K = Kirche/church
T = Turm/tower
W = Wasserstelle/spring
Z = Zisterne/cistern

Zeichnung: W. Herrmann

ally recognisable today, the one around the summit area. The wall is two-faced and made of medium-sized (30 – 40 cm) quarry stones set on one another basically in horizontal but not always symmetrical layers. Small stones serve to fill in the holes. Large stones were usually used for the spaces in between the two surfaces. The thickness of the walls is 2 – 3 m. In the northwest corner there are the remains of a semi-circular corner tower with an interior diameter of about 6 m. It is well preserved, just like the walls adjoining it on the exterior surface as a support for a terrain level several metres high. On the west side the remains of three flanking towers can be found: the northernmost is designed as a semi-circular tower while the two more to the south have a rectangular ground-plan. The gate are not preserved. Due to the position and the structure of the terrain, it can be assumed that the main gate might have been on the side facing the colony on the slope, where two building structures with well-cut wall edges made of quoins flank a three-metre-wide opening.

Within the precinct of the castle there are remains of mostly small buildings, few of which are preserved, with walls of small

elevation above the foundations. Some of them form a line run-
ning parallel to the surrounding wall on the western slope and
perhaps indicate a former row of streets; others stand individu-
ally on the narrow strip of the barely inclined summit. The orig-
inal form and purpose of the buildings are no longer recognis-
able. The cisterns are an exception, two of which on the west-
ern slope are especially remarkable. They were large water
reservoirs constructed above ground-level – recognisable by the
reddish clay mixture used in the coating of the walls – with care-
fully smoothed ground-level paved flooring and walls ascend-
ing like house walls (the height they actually reached is uncer-
tain). The in-flow of rainwater probably came from flat roofs
and possibly from a ground canal. The construction to the south
is about 26 m long and 5 m wide, the more northern construc-
tion is 22 m long and 5 m wide. Both were divided by partitions
and are characterised by careful wall-building techniques, the
largest and, with their walls still standing several metres high,
best preserved constructions in the castle area.

Near the semi-circular tower in the north-west there is another,
but differently constructed, cistern about 12 m long and 3 m
wide. Its receiving basin is worked into the ground, only the bar-
rel-vaulted roof extends above the ground. Along the east wall
several small cisterns built into the ground indicate that they
could have served to supply the inhabitants of individual build-
ings. A natural, if also limited, supply of water is available, a
damming-up of water in a rocky ground pit whose entryway was
walled up in rectangular form.

In the more northern part of the fortress, near the border to the
east, there are the ruins of a small church with two naves of dif-
ferent size. The larger nave has a wide breadth of 4 m, but the
length can no longer be clearly reconstructed (at least 12 m).

The smaller nave is almost 3 m wide and 8 m long. Two semi-circular apses were covered by half-domes, while the naves were vaulted with oblong barrel-vaults. On the southern side of the church, set back to the west, there is an oblong addition about 3 m wide with a length that can no longer be determined. It also has a semi-circular apse which apparently served as a chapel.

Return by the same route you came.

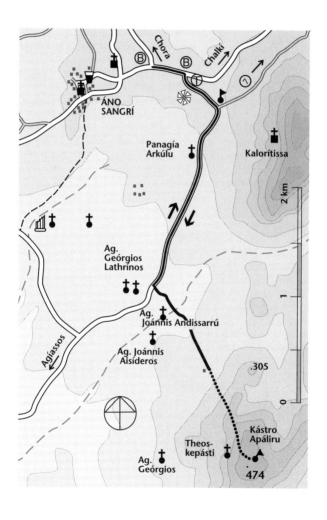

⑪ Apáno Kástro – The Upper Castle

As a counterpoint to the Kástro in the city of Náxos,
the Venetians called their main fortress in the in-
terior of the island the Upper Castle (Castel d'Alto).
The first step for this tour is to go to Chalkí by bus.
From there you will need three to four hours, along
very pleasant paths, to reach Potamiá. A roman-
tic garden taverna under shady trees and next to a
spring awaits you at your goal. The return trip to
Náxos by taxi must be organised from there, or you
can extend the walking tour with ⑬.

From the bus stop in **Chalkí** (GPS N 37° 03' 46.7" E 25° 28' 58.4")
cross through the village in a southwest direction to the road to
Tsikkalarió (Τσικκαλαρειό) or Potamiá. About 300 m after the end
of the village, 50 m to the right of the road, there is the chapel
of Agía Paraskeví (see ⑦ ⬜) (N 37° 03' 48.9" E 25° 28' 35.3").
From here a pleasant old trail leads, first to the right and
then to the left, up to **Tsikkalarió** (red markings). It leads past
the church of **Ágios Stéphanos** (¹/₂ hr/N 37° 03' 50.5" E 25° 28'
19.0"; closed) through Tsikkalarió towards the west (Odós Kástro,
Οδός Κάστρο). Then it goes uphill and leads through a wild, rocky
landscape to the east side of the fortress of Apáno Kástro. At the
chapel of **Ágios Pantelímonas** ⬜ (³/₄ hr/ N 37° 04' 02.3" E 25°
27' 44.6") go up the slope to the left. A sign shortly after the
chapel shows the name Tsikalariou Castle. The climb isn't easy
on any side. On the southern side, steep trampled paths lead up
to the **castle of Apáno Kástro** (1 hr).
From the top you can appreciate the dominating position of this
fortress. Far to the northwest there is the city of Náxos, nearer,
in a valley to the west, is Potamiá – our goal. You can recognise
the way from Tsikkalarió to Potamiá quite well from above. The
entire Tragéa plateau stretches out in the east. The villages of
Moní, Filóti, Chalkí, Damariónas and Damalás, with their white
buildings, almost disappear in the velvet green of the olive
groves. Sangrí is to the south-west.
In "Byzantine Castles on the Cyclades" Hannalene Eberhard
writes about this castle:

> *"Apáno Kástro was probably built about the middle of the 13th*
> *century. Because of its location at a greater altitude than that*
> *of the fortress of Náxos-Chora, it was called (Italian) "Castel*
> *d'Alto", in Greek Apano Kastro (Απάνω Κάστρο). Its main pur-*

pose was to protect the valuable agricultural land in the central region of Náxos, which can be controlled from the summit of the hill, as well as to survey and secure the connection between the harbour in the west and the fairly densely populated district in the interior, with a number of villages.

The castle consists of an outer fortification and a main fortress. The outer fortification spreads on the broad southern slope of the mountain. Its surrounding wall is preserved only in segments and cannot be recognised any more in its entire course or in its connection with the rocks in the east and west. The most prominent element of this outer enclosure is a horseshoe-shaped barbican, probably meant for the defence of an entrance gate, leaning against the slope with its straight line, while its rounded part projects outwards. The building is preserved in a height of 9m up to the highest point of its contact with the slope and also measures 9 m in diameter, including its thick walls. There are three loop-holes (fire-slits) in one of the lower floors and six in an upper one. Since the barbican has been built with slightly scarped walls, it must have been built later, at a time when fire arms were already in use.

Nothing remains of the gate as such. Within the outer works we find only a few traces of houses, which evidently means that there was no civil settlement, no "borgo" attached to the castle. The large enclosed circuit may, however, have served as a refuge for people from the neighbouring villages in case of danger.

A certain extent of ancient wall on the southwest slope, distinguishable from mediaeval walls by its big, evenly cut rectangular blocks, obviously belongs to the classical Greek period. As there are no other remains of the same type of masonry, it can be assumed that there existed only some sort of small fortification, possibly a watch-tower.

The castle proper occupies the mountain plateau. To a great deal its surrounding wall can be discerned, partly only in its foundations, along the edges of the plateau. It runs mostly in straight, angle-turn lines; only for a certain distance on the north side it forms a wide outward-curve. The space enclosed by this wall is 120 meters long; its greatest width is about 50 m.

Within the area of the main castle we find the remains of several separate buildings. Most conspicuous are those in the western sector, which seem to belong to a former church; three outer walls, with round arches, are preserved to a height of 4 m.

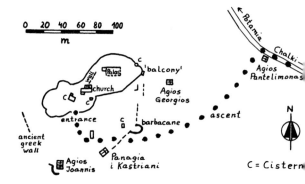

An extension added to the narrow eastern wall has not, as might be expected, the appearance of an apse, but is a rectangula niche, 1 m deep.

At a distance of 10 m northeast of this building, a certain extent of straight wall, actually consisting in a sequence of round arches partly broken down (2 m high), runs parallel to the northern enclosure. A great amount of fallen stones and debris behind the wall evidently are what is left of the building to which it once belonged.

Still further to the east are the ruins of the largest, centre building of the castle. Only its long northern wall is preserved to a height of 7 m, together with the northwest and northeast corners and very little of the adjoining west and east walls. The building was 20 m long, its exact width cannot be traced any more. Beyond the wall are some foundations of former partition walls. Underneath the northwest corner, now partly below the outer level, we see the only room of the entire castle which has remained intact. It measures 4 m x 3,50 m and is only 2 m high, with a ceiling consisting of two long barrel vaults supported by a big pillar in the middle. Possibly its function was that of a cistern.

The outline and the shape of the big building do not seem to coincide with those of a donjon, a keep; it is rather to be considered as the "Palas" of the castle, with rooms for living and for official, representative purposes.

At the eastern end of the surrounding wall a few steps, passing through a round arch, lead down to a small semicircular outer platform, called by the local people "The balcony of the Duchess". The existence of this balcony, with its view of the most beautiful scenery in the neighbourhood, as well as certain architectural elements in the sparse remains of the buildings of the castle, seems to indicate that it was not only meant for defence and military purposes, but was also supposed to be the noble home, the palace of the ducal family. As a matter of fact, the Greek people of Náxos do not use the word "Phrourion" (φρούριον) = "fortress" when they speak of the Apano Kastro, but rather call it "Palatia" (παλάτι) or "Anaktora" (ανακτορον), both meaning "palace."

Shortening the tour: If you would like to return to Chalkí, cross through the grounds of a prehistoric cemetery 400 m below the castle in the direction towards Chalkí. *The remains of the* **cemetery from the Geometric Epoch** *consist of about 50 prehistoric barrows (tumulus graves) and are mostly round and surrounded by uncut stones (diameter 5 to 12 m), but some are also rectangular. Excavations around 1963 showed that many graves had already been plundered, but interesting remains of burned bones, jewellery, ceramics and weapons were found. Some of these can be seen in the museum in the kástro of Náxos. At the entry to the field of graves there is a* **menhir** *about 2.5 m high*  *(N 37° 03' 49.6" E 25° 27' 53.2"). With a little skill, you can even find the remains of an ancient street leading through a small ravine to the plateau of the cemetery.*

From the west side of the fortified castle, go down past the remains of a very old cyclopean-like wall and then continue northwest across fields to the mule track leading from Chalkí to Potamiá, which you reach near the deteriorating grey stone chapel of **Ágios Andréas** (N 37° 04' 03.2" E 25° 27' 25.1"). Inside, however, you can still see lovely frescoes . Follow the old path, built by the Venetians and paved with large stones, to the west (red markings). Keep to this direction on the lane following it.

Shortly afterwards, cross the asphalt road going from Chalkí to
Potamiá (N 37° 04' 06.3'' E 25° 26' 54.3'') and go down the steps
then to the right and in a big curve to the left through **Áno
Potamiá** to get to the Taverne I Pigí (H ΠHΓH; The Spring) or Par
adise Garden, where you can eat and rest under shady trees.
From Áno – or Káto Potamiá, you can return by bus or taxi.
If you would like to walk on further to **Ágios Mámas**, you can
take a beautiful path described in the second section of ⑬.

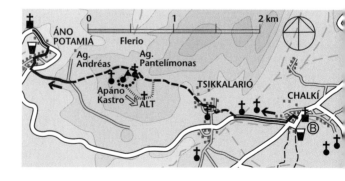

⑫ Kúros, the Youth

A three to four-hour trek to the colossal statue of the Kúros of Phlerio and then on to Mélanes. For the most part without defined paths, but the way is easy to find. Please note that there are just four and a half hours between the arrival of the first bus in Chalkí and the return journey from Kúros. It is necessary to enquire as to the bus times. At a push, you may have to call a taxi (Tel. 224 44).

Take the first bus to **Chalkí**, turn down the **lane** to the right o᠋ the kafeníon and go past the square and the attractive taverna᠋ Unfortunately, you don't have time today!

Head right on the road below, out of the village, and 300 m alon᠍ the road, between olive groves, up to a **bridge** with a small build᠋ing ①. Turn right here along a path and then left straight after᠋ up an idyllic way to the village of **Tsikkalarió**. On the edge o᠋ the village, there is a small church overlooking the plain o᠋ Tragéa. It is striking that many of the houses in this delightfu᠋ landscape have tiled roofs, the reason being that it rains quite᠋ often. The way through the houses is fairly flat. From the **end o᠍ the village** (¹/₄ hr) you can see the ruins of the mountain fortres᠍ of Apáno Kástro ② in the middle of a moonscape and come to ᠋ wall in a green valley above.

Alternative: If you climb up left in front of the wall, yo᠋ reach a plateau of rock.

*A **burial site** from Geometric times (750 BC) has been exca᠋ vated here. A rock stood on end, similar to a menhir, is visible᠋ and above it, Apáno Kástro ②. You can just make out som᠋ 30 circular or elliptical tombs, measuring up to twelve metre᠍*

*in diameter. The burial gifts found in the dolmen, including
ceramics, gold jewellery and charred figs and nuts, are on view
in a raised cabinet at the Museum of Archaeology in Chóra.*
To the *right* of the wall, a path leads up to the **chapel** (¹/₂-hour)
on the pass. From here you go on 200 m up to a small, hidden
doorway in the wall on the left.

*Those wanting to storm the fortress must climb up ten minutes
from here. The old Venetian Castel d'Alto, now **Apáno Kástro**,
lies in ruins and looks across to Náxos town and the island of
Páros. See* ⑪

From below the fortress, descend without a path through the
rocks to the Phlério plateau, which has something mystical about
it. Above a large rock, is a door in the fence, and to the left, a
place you can climb over it. Three rocks ③ are stood on the edge
of the valley, which is green in the spring. It's easy to find your
way along left of the oleander-lined creek and on the slope. The
castle guards the valley from behind. At the end of the valley, we
pass a walled field with wind-bent trees on the right. Across the
stream bed (1¹/₄ hr) and then later directly in the bed itself, the
going is slow between the oleander bushes. A fence has to be surmounted in the dry bed. It's best to stay in the stream bed until
it becomes a **concrete track** (1¹/₂ hr). A few hundred metres on
concrete follow, but under mighty trees with a wall of reeds along
the side.

> **Alternative:** When you see a rusty machine near a stone wall
> on the left, you can go up the lane to the left till you reach
> the fencing, cross diagonally through the field beyond it
> and come upon the **Kúros of Potamiá** ④ (N 37° 04'51,7''
> E 25° 27' 14,3'') upwards to the left on a small terrace, in
> the middle of clumps of rocks. This is the former marble

★

quarry, where half-hewn pillars and other architectural fragments can also be found.

Otherwise, continue along the concrete track under the trees until there are several signs pointing left. From the other direction they read: **Kúros of Phlério**, the youth in the garden! (1³/₄ hr)

> *Kúros statues represent gods or heroes. This prostrate statue dates from around the 6ᵗʰ century BC and was probably intended for the Holy Grove on Délos. It was never completed due to a flaw in the material and remained in this position in the ancient quarry.*
>
> *This Kúros belongs to the Kondili family, who also own the well-tended garden around it. You can order snacks and drinks.*

Having fortified yourself, head left from Kúros along the concrete track you came on, going up 600m to the bus stop at the crossing. However, there is no bus in the late afternoon!

> *Alternative:* If you prefer to walk to Mélanes and order a taxi there, head straight on over the crossing in the valley, along the concrete track which later becomes a dirt track. The **fork** to the left with the sign "Mélanes" is the wrong way; go *straight on* (towards the dead-end), around the hill, until Mélanes comes into view on the slope above a terraced valley a short time later. You arrive in the lower part of the rather austere village of **Mélanes**. There is an interesting view above the slope opposite: the summit has been carved up by human hand and borne away: marble from Kinídaros.

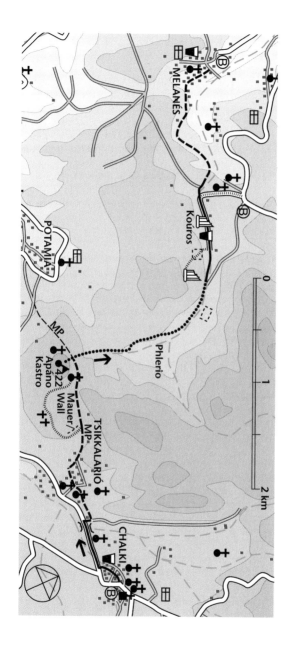

⑬ The Green Valley of Potamiá

This easy walking tour, large parts of which are under shady trees, is about eight kilometres long and takes six hours. It leads past the famous kúros of Mélanes, through the lovely valley of Potamiá, ending at the former residence of the Catholic bishops of Náxos. Along the way there are several places where you can stop and for refreshments. You can shorten the tour by taking the bus directly to the kúros.

Take a bus or taxi to the village of **Mélanes**, sector **Ágii Apóstoli** (GPS N 37° 05' 27.7'' E 25° 26' 18.9''). Begin on the main street and walk into the village towards the south. In front of the village church Ágii Apóstoli turn to the left (ΟΔΟΣ ΑΓ. ΑΠΟΣ-ΤΟΛΩΝ) and after 150 m again to the right.

Follow the lane along the slope here, where you have a good view out over the fertile Mélanes valley. Olive trees as well as orange and lemon plantations bear testimony to the intensive agricultural use. The ruins of several watermills can be made out. Many cypress trees contribute to the special character of this valley. On the opposite side of the valley, there are the villages of Kurunochóri, with the Venetian tower pírgos della Rókka, and the hamlet Míli. The white chapel Ágios Geórgios is in the valley. The way leads you along the valley.

After crossing the slope in a big arc, you can see the white chapel Ypapantí to the south.

Another 300 m further along, you meet up with a cross-road which you should follow to the left towards the east. Cross over a stream through the oleander bushes, and you will come to the connecting asphalt road leading from the main street down to the kúros. The bus stops here, too.

Go along the cemented stretch of this road to the south for 200 m, between shady oleander bushes, plane-trees, cypresses and olive trees. A sign on the right side near a garden gate indicates the way to the **Kúros of Flério** ① (³/₄ hr/N 37° 05' 00.5' E 25° 27' 07.5'').

> *Kúros statues represent ancient gods or heroes. The name means "youth". Statues of females, such as on the Akropolis in Athens are called Kores*
> *The over 6-metre-long kúros from the 6ᵗʰ century B.C. was probably left in half-completed condition due to its broken leg.*

A second, more poorly preserved kúros is found about 300 m higher up, to the southeast. You can find it as in ⑫ or as described further on.

From the kúros a small gate leads into a delightful garden of paradise with fruit trees, flower beds and vegetable cultures. You can get something simple to eat and drink and sit, in a classically rustic way, on a wooden bench under a gnarled old olive tree near a goldfish pond.

To continue wandering, return to the beginning of the cement

strip. A narrow pass upwards to the left begins there (N 37° 05′ 02.2″ E 25° 27′ 00.9″; red markings).

> *Alternative:* After about ten minutes a sign indicates the way to the **Kúros of Potamiá** to the left. There are some markings on the path which first leads past a pen on the left and then through two field walls. You walk about ¼ hour from the main way, following the contour lines until you find the statue. (photo ⑫) (N 37° 04′ 51.7″ E 25° 27′ 14.3″). You can look for fragments of pillars in this former quarry.

After a short time you can recognise the ruins of the former Venetian fortification Apáno Kástro on a mountain peak to the southeast. Beyond it, the peak of Mount Zeus can be seen. In the spring, observant wanderers can discover a lot of orchids along the edge of the path.

The path turns to the right after about 1 km and then to the left after another 300 m. Red and blue dots are helpful for orientation. On past the cemetery in Potamiá and the church of Ágios Ioánnis, you finally come to **Áno Potamiá**, where the shady taverna Η ΠΗΓΗ (The Spring) (2 hrs/N 37° 04′ 12.8″ E 25° 26′ 58.4″) awaits you for an extended rest. You can return from here by taxi.

From Áno Potamiá you start off again to the south (Odós Emman. M. Giampura, ΟΔΟΣ ΕΜΜΑΝ. Μ. ΓΙΑΜΠΟΥΡΑ) through the village and then turn to the right downhill to the river. Cross it on the bridge and walk along the slope on a very nice paved path (see page 65), without going down to the valley with its fruit gardens.

On past the school in **Mési Potamiá**, you easily reach **Káto Potamiá** (2³/₄ hrs/ N 37° 04' 0.6" E 25° 26' 02.2"). In the summer there is a wonderfully shady cafe on the terrace below the church (Panagía). *Before* the church go down to the south towards the river (Odós Agiú Nikódimu, ΟΔΟΣ ΑΓΙΟΥ ΝΙΚΟΔΗΜΟΥ) cross over it on the bridge and follow the arrows pointing to the church of Ágios Mámas, uphill and then downhill. The beautiful

★ path leads around the slope in a wide arc. After a stream which might be hard to cross after a strong rainfall, turn to the right and you will arrive at the church of **Ágios Mámas** ② (3¹/₄ hrs/N 37° 03' 37.5" E 25° 25' 41.8"). You might possibly have to climb over walls or hedges first.

> *The church, dating back to at least the 9th century A.D., was originally orthodox but became Catholic in the Middle Ages. With some effort you can still find some frescoes in the half restored church. The structure located somewhat above the church served intermittently as a summer residence for the Catholic bishops and has now been leased to a farmer.*

From Ágios Mámas, go up to the west across the fields past the former bishop's palace. About 100 m above this building and behind a wall there is a dirt road which you should follow to the right for 100 to 200 m. Pass the lovely entry gate to the grounds: in the eighties there still used to be a small spring here. Due to the pumping of deep water, it has dried up, and many of the orange trees have died.

An old mule track begins at the gate, going first to the north and then up to left to the **road** (4 hrs/ N 37° 03' 39.6" E 25° 25' 13.8") where you can wave down the bus to Náxos – if it isn't too full. In half an hour, on the right of the road to Náxos (easy but boring) or along small paths and the edges of fields, you come to the **Pírgos Belónia**, which was restored privately in 1986 and is now accessible to the public (4¹/₂ hrs/N 37° 04' 13.8" E 25° 24' 46.6") directly on the main road. Next to the pírgos there is one of the double churches typical for Náxos: the right half of the Ágios Ioánnis is Orthodox, the left Catholic. From there it is only a few minutes to **Galanádo**, where you can wait for the bus more comfortably with a cup of coffee.

⑭ The Jesuit Cloister

This easy circular walking tour through the fertile Mélanes Valley can be completed comfortably in three hours. You come in contact with the ruins of a forsaken cloister and walk along a shady path to the small village of Kurunochóri. There are several pleasant possibilities to stop for refreshments along the six-kilometre stretch.

Take the bus to the village of **Mélanes** (sector Ágii Apóstoli; GPS N 37° 05′ 27.9″ E 25° 26′ 18.5″). From the bus stop, you have a lovely view into the Mélanes Valley. On the opposite side, there is the village of Kurunochóri, in the middle of which you can see, with a bit of effort, the brown-grey Venetian tower-house Pírgo della Rokka. Take the way south through the village to the village church. Continue past the tavernas with their very creative advertising signs, then slightly diagonally to the right and about 100 m up steps to a road which is cement at the beginning. After about 400 m you reach a flat ridge with several dirt roads branching off from it. Signs to Kouros/Kalamitsia Κουρος/Καλα-

★ μιτσια indicate the next dirt road on the way to the **cloister of Kalamitsia** (also Kalamitsa; ³/₄ hr/N 37° 04′ 42.5″ E 25° 26′ 15.0″), about 500 m away.

> *Kalamítsia was built by the French Jesuit Robert Saulger in the 17th century as a cloister for the members of his order, probably on the ruins of a former ducal palace. Saulger wrote a very detailed history of Náxos. A large garden, now overgrown with blackberry bushes, was planted. The Jesuits used to cultivate the land intensively. This led, however, to constant disputes with less successful domestic farmers.*

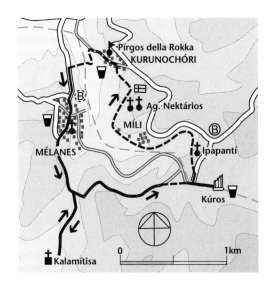

In 1773 Lazarists took over the building. In 1877 it was passed
on to the Salesians, who ran it until 1927. Today the decaying
property belongs to the state.
There are plans for its reconstruction and even for building an
expensive hotel.

From Kalamítsia, first return via the same dirt road you came on.
Then, at the sign to the kúros, follow the dirt road leading uphill
in curves to the east. Along this you have a direct view of the impressive marble mining in the mountains.
About 800 m after the sign, a mule path turns off to the right at
a sharp angle and leads directly down to the river bed. Beyond
this, the asphalt road leading to the kúros can be recognised.
Down at the place where the asphalt road changes to a cemented section (1¹/₂ hrs/N 37° 5′ 2.8″ E 25° 27′ 1.1″) you come to the
Kúros of Flério ⑬ in the southwest. Here you can enter here into a delightful garden of paradise with fruit trees, flower beds and
vegetable cultures. You can get something simple to eat and drink
and sit under old olive trees near a goldfish pond.
If you have already visited the kúros, turn north on the asphalt
road. After a few metres, a path branches off the road to the left
at a sharp angle. It leads to the white-washed **church of Ypapantí**, whose three interior rooms have been restored.
Continue along a trampled path next to electricity wires until

you reach a cemented way leading downhill to the left. After about 550 m you pass the small village of **Míli** (1³/₄ hrs/N 37 5' 14.6" E 25° 26' 45.8"). The fertility of this region can clearly be seen in the many gardens and fields whose water provision has been assured through very old rights. The nice, shady path leads on past the double church of Ágios Nektários to the village of **Kurunochóri** (2 ¹/₂ hrs/N 37° 5' 37.9" E 25° 26' 32.9").

> *Opposite the main church of Metamórfosis tu Sotíros, there is a large round marble table* ② *in a somewhat lower private garden which, however, is usually accessible, with an engraving in French recalling the visit of the young Greek-Bavarian King Otto in the year 1833.*
>
> *A Venetian **pírgos** is also near the church. It belongs to the della Rokka family and is closed. The characteristic construction of this manor house can, nevertheless, be recognised easily from the outside.*

From here go down small alleys and steps to the valley, where a lovely old cypress-lined walk leads back to **Mélanes**. Now it is not far to the road and the bus stop.

⑮ The Olive Groves of the Tragéa

This easy 2-hour walk leads through the largest olive groves on Náxos, past an interesting potter's workshop and a restored oil mill and on to a very special double church. And after five kilometres, a wonderful shady taverna awaits you!

Have the bus driver stop at the **bus stop Damalás** on the main road Náxos – Chalkí (GPS N 37° 03' 18.1'' E 25° 28' 03.1'') and walk along the road to Damalás for about 440 m until you reach Damalás. At the beginning of the village you come to the **ceramic workshop** of Manólis Libertas, who makes not only ceramics for daily use but also individual forms of pottery. A speciality from Náxos is a storage vessel called "potíri thikiosini" ①-left. A comparatively normal-looking drinking cup called "potíri pitágora" has a surprise in store. Manólis enjoys showing both items and, of course, selling them, too.

> *In Damalás itself, there is a very nicely renovated old oil mill only 50 m to the right of the way described below (1/2 hr/N 37° 03' 04.0'' E 25° 28' 08.8''). If it should be shut, you can ask Manólis at the pottery shop. There and in the oil mill, a little leaflet is available (Yiannis S. Veronis: The traditional olive-press of Damalas) which explains the history and use of the equipment.*

After a short walk further into the village, turn left into the Odós Ag. Irínis (ΟΔΟΣ ΑΓ. ΕΙΡΗΝΗΣ). The way leads to the southeast first, uphill through the village and on to the church of **Agía Iríni** 3/4 hr./N 37° 03' 04.9'' E 25° 28' 20.0'').

A partially cemented dirt road leads on past the church to Damariónas. At the beginning of the village, *don't* take the as-

phalt street down to the left, but instead go straight ahead in the small alleys. (Photo ⑨ ③) You will come to the church of Christós or Metamórphosis tu Sotíros (Christ's Transfiguration). In the churchyard there is a bust of Ioánnis K. Paparigópulos (1 hr N 37° 03' 09.5" E 25° 28' 46.5"), who distinguished himself on the mainland in 1821 during the battle for independence against the Turks.

Continue on through the twisting lanes of Damariónas north-east to east until you come to a road leading to Filotí above the village school. Follow this for a while.

From here you have a wide view over the Tragéa plateau. Villages are hidden in the vast olive groves, and only their white churches and grey towers, the pírgi, stand out. To the west, the Venetian castle Apáno Kástro ⑪ towers up.

One kilometre after Damariónas, turn off to the left to the white-washed chapel **Tímios Stavrós** (1¹/₂ hrs/N 37° 03' 17.3" E 25° 29' 31.2"). A dirt road leads past it to the north. After another 200 m, a small path turns off to the left (red markings).

After a short while, through partially overgrown and dark, narrow passages cut through the olive groves, you reach the church of **Ágii Apóstoli** ② (1³/₄ hrs/N 37° 03' 37.1" E 25° 29' 14.1") which is unfortunately closed. It dates back to about the 10th century and is distinguished by its unusual construction with a second chapel built on top above the entry. Diagonally across there is the **church of Agía Eleúsa** or Metochiótissa, from the 17th century.

From Ágii Apóstoli, take a narrow path to the west, which soon becomes a dirt road. After about 400 m, a wide path turns off to the right (sign KTHMA Γ. MAMOYZEΛOY; property of Mamuzelos) and then stops after 100 m. Hardly perceptible among the olive groves about 50 m away, there is the natural-stone-coloured Byzantine chapel **Ágios Geórgios** (2¹/₄ hrs/ N 37° 03' 40.0" E 25° 28' 55.5").

From here, follow the tracks to the north-west which lead to a more distinct path. With a little skill, you will find red marking leading to Chalkí.

In the old village centre of **Chalkí**, there is the typically Greek taverna belonging to "Jannis", where you can revive yourself wonderfully under shady trees. A visit to the near-by distillery Vallindras, where the special Naxian liqueur kitron made of citrus fruits is produced, is worth your time. The main church on the street is also extremely interesting. Unfortunately, it is closed very often.

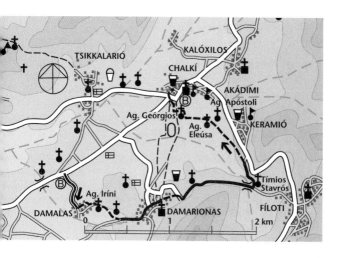

▷ Publications of Local Organizations

The mayor of the new administrative district Drimália has published a nice brochure with walking tours in the central part of Náxos:

Central Náxos, A Guide with Map, Municipality of Drimália, 2001

This brochure is available in English and Greek.

A similar brochure is also currently being prepared for the area around Kóronos.

⑯ Dream Paths

This classical walking tour is a 'must'. It reveals the fertile Tragéa plains in the interior of Náxos and brings you in contact with Byzantine chapels, Venetian residence towers and picturesque villages. It is over seven kilometres and takes about five hours. Along the way, attractive tavernas invite you to have a rest and take refreshment.

At the bus stop in **Chalkí** (GPS N 37° 03′ 46.7″ E 25° 28′ 58.4″) there is the main church **Panagía i Evangelístria 'I Protótronos'** (The Virgin on the Highest Throne). It contains impressive frescoes in the interior and is absolutely worth seeing. You must ask the Papás for the key if it doesn't happen to be open. He is very happy for any small contribution.

The way begins to the left of the church and heads towards the closed **Pírgos Grazía** ① almost next to it. A coat of arms of the Venetian family Barózzi hangs over the entry gate. 200 m further on past the pírgos, in the next settlement called Akádimi, there is the **Pírgos Markopolíti** or **Papadáki**, which is also closed. The pírgi were the fortified residences of Venetian families during the Middle Ages.

A little bit further to the west, there is the chapel Ágios Nikólaos with its red-tiled roof. Cross the road Chalkí-Filóti here and head to the north. You pass an old oil mill which is no longer used and, several minutes later, reach Kalóxilos.

On past the main church in **Kalóxilos**, Agía Triáda, (¼ hr/N 37 03′ 55.7″ E 25° 29′ 20.4″), go through the village to the north. It is easy to lose your way here. At the end of the village, you should pass two chapels located next to one another, Agii Apóstoli (ΑΓΙΟΙ ΑΠΟΣΤΟΛΟΙ) and Agía Ekaterína (ΑΓΙΑ ΑΙΚΑΤΕΡΙΝΑ) and also a cemetery to the right of the path. Red and blue dots mark the foot path heading north to northeast. It begins going gently uphill and becomes a bit steeper and rockier later on. From the rounded hill-top you can see the village of Moní to the north. The magnificent view behind you looks out upon the Tragéa plateau around Chalkí, covered with olive trees. The old word for Tragéa was Drymalia, which is now the term for the administrative district in the middle of Náxos. About half of the approximately 400,000 olive trees on Náxos are here.

Parts of the path lead you on newly made vehicle tracks, making orientation on the original trails more difficult. It is two kilome tres to Moní. Along the way you will see the sign '**Wood Work-shop**' (³/₄ hr). The carpenter Michael Kontopidis has set up his workshop directly on the path. He sells artistic works in wood as well as weavings (N 37° 04' 39.7'' E 25° 29' 46.6''). And perhaps, under the shady oaks, he will also offer you a glass of the wine he has pressed himself.

North of here, after wandering through a deep, fertile valley, you reach the village of **Moní** (1 ¹/₄ hrs/N 37° 04' 55.0'' E 25° 29' 47.7''), known for its lovely hand-woven goods which are often

shown in exhibitions. Several shady tavernas with a view of the valley offer an invitation to a well-earned lunch.

In Moní, continue on through the village towards the west and look for a small path downhill to the southwest. The church we are looking for can be seen from here. After about 150 m, near a fork, turn to the right. Shortly before the road, to the right between olive trees, there is the church **Panagía i Drosianí** ② (Virgin Fresh as Dew, also called Drosani) (2 hrs./N 37° 04' 52.2'' E 25° 29' 35.4'').

> *The church probably dates back to the 6ᵗʰ century A.D. and is composed of several agglomerated chapels built next to one another. It is famous for its excellently restored frescoes from the 6ᵗʰ or 7ᵗʰ century A.D. Frescoes which were later painted over these in the 13ᵗʰ and 14ᵗʰ centuries were removed in a thorough restoration between 1964 and 1971. The church is normally open in the high season and the time directly before and after. If it should be closed, ring the church doorbell several times and wait for some minutes until someone comes to open the door. A small contribution is appropriate. Picture-taking is not permitted, but there are postcards and a little leaflet (English and Greek) about the history of the church.*

Continue by crossing the asphalt road before Drosianí and go downhill on the opposite side to get to a stream bed which is usually dry. Don't go through the gate on the side marked with a red circle! Walk *in* the stream bed to the left (red markings help occasionally). The rest of the way continues on the left next to the stream until you reach a spot with some steps leading downhill and red dots (2 ½ hrs/N 37° 04' 37.5'' E 25° 29' 15.9'').

From the steps, continue along a shady narrow pass to the stream bed. Follow this for 300 m and then go upwards diagonally from the stream bed (a cairn, a little pile of stones, is possibly there as a marking). Now go along this path and then turn off it uphill to the right after 300 m. Now you come to the chapel **Panagía i Rachidiótissa** ③ (2³/₄ hrs/N 37° 04' 23.8'' E 25° 29' 03.7''). Unfortunately, it is closed, but this is a nice place for a break.

★ Then go downhill to the west for 80 m and turn left at the fork. A very nice narrow pass leads through a sparse oak forest. On the opposite slope you can see the deteriorating basilica Ágios Isídoros with its three naves. At the beginning of the village of **Monítsa** (Rachí), on the right side of the path, there is the chapel two-nave chapel Ágios Nikólaos (3 hrs/N 37° 04' 06.9'' E 25° 28' 54.0''). 50 m further on a view opens up down into the valley to the half-deteriorated chapel O Taxiárchis, and then you pass the chapel Ágios Antónios with its marble-tiled roof.

Leave Monítsa, which almost always presents a drowsy impression, to the southeast and cross over a stream. A dirt road begins at the bridge. Take it for about 100 m but then go straight ahead at the sharp curve to the left, following the signs to the Ágios Diassorítis. After 300 m you come upon **Ágios Geórgios o Diassorítis**, St George the Saviour ④ in the midst of olive trees (3¹/₄ hrs/N 37° 03' 57.8'' E 25° 28' 50.6''; open daily except Mon

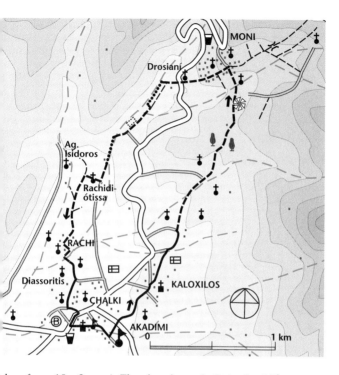

days from 10 – 2 p.m.). The church was built in the 11th century and is characterised by especially abundant frescoes.

James T. Bent wrote the following about the churches in Chalkí in 1883:

> "Chalkí seems to have been a place of considerable importance in mediaeval days, and the Church of St. John (Protótronis) here is the oldest Christian building on the island: it is curious in formation, with a long porch with three Gothic arches on either side, about fifty feet long, and having no roof to it now, but a vine trailing over it; this seems to be a mediaeval addition. Inside, the building is strictly Byzantine; you enter a narrow narthex with arches on either side which lead into two dark collateral chapels; between the narthex and the choir is a narrow space with a waggon roof; over the choir is a dome covered with frescoes. The front of this church has a stepped edging. All around Chalkí are ruins of churches, dating from the Middle Ages, hidden away and buried in the olive groves; one of them,

dedicated to St. George (Diassorítis), is especially picturesque, being covered with ivy, and over the archway into the nave is a very long old Hellenic inscription; also there are several traces of an ancient temple – perhaps that of Apollon Trajios."

To get to Chalkí, follow the signs and markings. In a lovely spot in the old village centre of **Chalkí** there is taverna "Jannis", a favourite with wanderers. It is pleasant to wait a while for the bus while sitting at a table in the shade.

St. Nikolaos Sangri

Rural Chapels and Icons

Small chapels, usually owned by farmers, are characteristic in the Greek countryside. The ceiling is covered with flat beams or made of barrel-vaulted masonry. Larger churches with a dome above a cruciform ground plan are called "cruciform-domed churches".

In front is a lovingly cared-for spot with a bench and often, in a tree, a bell. This is where the consecration of the church, the "Panigíri", is celebrated with song and dance every year on the date of the church's patron saint. The interior is simple: cement pavement as the floor, cleansing equipment, candles, sand glass, matches. Usually there is a little oil lamp burning, encouraging the traveller to engage in thought.

The altar wall is opposite the door, with the iconostasis made of lacquered wood and icons in the compartments. A representation of the patron saint is to the right. The room behind, the "Bema", should only be entered by the priest.

Sometimes there is pathetic naive icon painting, but often only printed representations of the saints. The **painting of icons** used to be reserved for priests and was considered a part of the liturgy. Even today the colours and composition are set exactly, making a differentiation of the time painted hardly possible. The person represented, with his eyes wide open, is removed from time. Only few buildings, landscapes and representations in perspective can be found. The icons, painted on wooden panels and then covered with a layer of linseed oil, are often covered, except for the faces, with a veneer of embossed silver. They are durable, can be kissed and touched as often as desired and even, according to church sagas, can withstand longer periods of time in holes in the ground. The founding of many churches is based on an icon found in the countryside or sea.

The old **frescoes** treat the same theme. Frescoes in ceiling domes normally represent Christ as the Pantokrator, the Lord of the World. God the Father is represented in the form of angels. The an-iconic frescoes from the time of the dispute about images in the 8th century are a speciality. Since illustrated representation of saints was forbidden at times, geometric and floral motifs were used. Especially interesting illustrations can be admired in ㉒.

⑰ Steep Ascent to Zeus

Today it becomes more mountainous – an attempt to mount the steep west side of the highest mountain of the Cyclades. For this you should choose a clear day. On the way to the peak, you pass a cave that requires a good flashlight for exploration. For the peak it is advisable to have windproof clothing. There are several springs along the way. The trip takes four hours.

At the bus stop in **Filóti** (GPS N 37° 3' 7.7" E 25° 29' 53.1"), you can already pick out a taverna for the return and continue along the main road about 700 m slightly uphill in the direction of Apírantos/Apóllon. At the mini-chapel on the right-hand side of the road, turn right in the direction of Chimarrós/Kalandós.

> *Alternative:* 250 m after the mini chapel, you will find a beaten track, up to the left, to the dominating **white domed church** (N 37° 2' 39.3" E 25° 29' 31.8") of Agía Iríni from 1995. From here, go along the asphalt road to the right around the hill and slowly uphill. The landscape becomes greener, and the asphalt road ends at a car park. Further up, you will quickly find the resting place.

After about 500 m along the road, just before a mill (¹/₂ hr/N 37° 2' 42.4" E 25° 29' 21.8"), go up onto a path which turns off the road at a sharp angle and is hardly recognisable at first. The path goes closely behind past the mill, becomes more noticeable and lovelier and ends after a big semicircle southwards at an inviting shady **resting place** with a spring (🔲 (³/₄ hr/N 37° 2' 10.9" E 25° 29' 37.6").

From here, a path, in good condition at the beginning and later becoming a marked, beaten track, leads uphill and past another

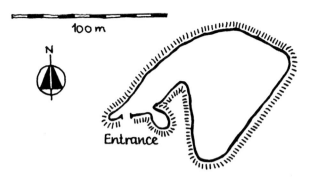

100 m

N

Entrance

spring to the **Cave of Zeus** (1 hr/N 37° 2′ 4.7″ E 25° 29′ 57.8″).
Legend has it that this was the god's birthplace. There are, however, other places that claim this, too.

> The cave is damp, at first flat inside but then quickly becomes
> stony and slippery.
>
> Entering the 150 m deep cave alone and without a good flash-
> light is dangerous. Bats live here; other occupants are big yel-
> low spiders. An earlier use was reported by the Royal Saxon
> Mountain Commissioner Fiedler: "It is said that orgies were
> celebrated in this grotto; actually it would have been the best
> place to bring raged humans to their senses; only the front part
> was said to have been used for this; so there are not many raged
> persons on Náxos"

The stony path then leads on uphill and comes to a **patch of
rubble** and loose stones (1¼ hr/N 37° 2′ 1.7″ E 25° 30′ 2.7″).

> **Alternative:** *Experienced* climbers can also climb directly up
> the patch of rubble. Quite high up the patch of rubble, turn
> at a break to the left and you will come to the easy uphill
> part of the mountain crest.

Otherwise, go steeply uphill to the left to a fence with a wall. In
this area a certain amount of sure-footing is called for. The grand
view compensates for the difficult progress.

At the fence, turn to the right and follow it. It soon leads to the
left, and it becomes tight between the fence and the rock face
pushing from the right. When the fence leads downwards to the
left, you can see your intermediate goal on a hill above to the
right: one or two stone towers about two metres in height.
Carry on uphill using the unmarked goat track until you come
to the small **stone towers**. From here you will see the mountain peak to the right and also the trodden paths leading

there. Blue and red dots, although sometimes faded, mark the way.

> *The Peak of Zas (2 hrs/N 37° 1′ 49.3″ E 25° 30′ 8.2″) is marked by a cement block with signs placed there by an Italian topographer. You have reached the highest point of the Cyclades, 1001 m above sea level and 600 m higher than Filóti. To the southeast the tower of Chimárru* ⑱ *is hardly visible, to the northeast is the monastery of Fotodótis* ⑲. *Goose vultures can frequently be seen flying around the peak at a respectable distance.*

> *The German archeologist Ernst Curtius was here in 1839: „I sat for a good hour on the very top stone of the mountain of Zeus and saw delightedly the rich island below me and the whole expanse of the sea of islands." He counted 44 islands as far as Turkey and, I suppose, had better visibility than we nowadays.*

At first the descent is the same way in reverse, but later leads downhill to the right in a northeast direction and then to the east for a while. Red and blue dots as well as cairns (mounds of stones) mark the way. Past the remains of two old **round chalk ovens** which look like oversized wells (2¹/₂ hrs/N 37º 02′ 18.6″ E 25º 30′ 46.5″), walk down a marble path to the northwest in steep serpentines and pass a **watering place** (2³/₄ hrs/N 37º 02′ 22.7″ E 25º 30′ 35.3″) which may have run dry by mid-summer. An ancient inscription carved in overhanging stone appears: ΟΡΟΣ ΔΙΟΣ ΜΗΛΩΣΙΟΥ ② (Mountain of Zeus, Protector of the

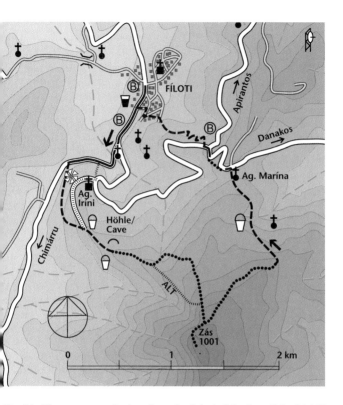

Herds). Then you reach the **chapel of Agía Marína** (3 hr/N 37°
02′ 41.7″ E 25° 30′ 25.6″) and the road to Danakós.
Follow this road to the left and later cleverly shorten the serpentine curves by taking direct paths. At the **junction** (N 37° 02′
47.0″ E 25° 30′ 14.2″) into the Filóti–Apírantos road, go to the
left and then after about 50 m to the right to climb down the
beautiful step-causeway to **Filóti** (3¹/₂ hr). There lovely tavernas
will be waiting for you.

⑱ The lonely Tower

*The slightly strenuous five-hour walk leads through
lonely countryside to a very well-preserved fortified
tower which dates from the Hellenic time. A good
sense of direction is imperative for this route of over
eight kilometres, as paths are not always available.
Return to Filóti best by taxi or hitchhike (Taxi in
Filóti: 228 50-313 28/ 752 82). The journey on foot
would take an additional three hours.*

The bus stops upon request beyond Filóti at the **junction to
Danakós**; (GPS N 37° 02' 47.0'' E 25° 30' 14.2''). Follow this road
upwards 400 m – the serpentines can be shortened when walking – to the chapel of **Agía Marína** (¹/₄ hr/N 37° 02' 41.7'' E 25°
30' 25.6''), which stands to the right of the road on the pass. A
footpath begins from the narrow path by the chapel and winds
slowly uphill. Red signs marked with "2" show the way. After 500
m you come to a **watering place** (¹/₂ hr/N 37° 02' 22.7'' E 25°
30' 35.3'') which is often dry in mid-summer. Near this spring an
inscription in ancient Greek is carved in overhanging marble:
ΟΡΟΣ ΔΙΟΣ ΜΗΛΩΣΙΟΥ (Mountain of Zeus, Protector of the
Herds).
Afterwards, the path winds upwards in steep serpentines and becomes slightly vague. In case of doubt, keep mounting higher.
After 800 m you reach the remains of two old round **chalk ovens**
with a diameter of about four metres (³/₄ hr/N 37° 02' 18.6''
E 25° 30' 46.5''). To get to the *top of the Zeus* you turn to the *right*;
all red dots lead to the peak.
A very visible trail leads straight ahead to the south to southeast.
A high wall is to the right. After passing through a gate, continue to the left. You will seldom see anyone here. Altogether you
will walk five kilometres, at times without a path, slightly up and
downhill in the same direction. Generally, keep to the slope at
about the same height or slightly downwards. By no means
should you, however, go too deep down into a valley.
After some time you will have a panoramic view of the small islands lying in front of Náxos, the so-called Erimonísia. To the
south is Iráklia, next to it to the east are Schinoússa, Káto and
Áno Koufoníssia and, on beyond, Kéros. Moreover, about a kilometre in the distance you will see a small chapel and several tracks
leading to it. This is the intermediate destination, reachable, how-

ever, only with a few detours. You have to pass through a large group of trees in a gorge and a few pens as well as gates made out of steel mesh. On a slightly ascending dirt track, you reach the **Chapel of Ágios Ioánnis** (3 hrs/N 37° 01′ 21.6″ E 25° 30′ 52.6″). From here, go down to the southeast a little further along the dirt track diagonally to the left. At the first turn, leave the dirt track and go to the right towards the south-southwest. In the distance you will now see the next intermediate goal, a flat saddle of a hill, 1.5 kilometres as the crow flies. Again, this is unable to be reached in a straight line. After going around a deep gorge with relatively dense woods in a big semicircle, you reach the **flat saddle**

(3³/₄ hrs/N 37° 00′ 26.2″ E 25° 31′ 01.0″). It is indicated on the map between 523 m and 524 m. From here, 1.5 kilometres to the southeast, you can see the tower, which does not stand out very much from the surroundings. On a clear day some of the southern Cyclades are visible once again: Irákia, Ios and, on beyond, Santoríni.

The asphalt road coming from Filóti runs west to east, past the tower to Kalandós in the south of the island. From the flat saddle, go down southwest to the road, where you turn left to the **Tower of Chimárru** ① (4¹/₂ hrs/N 36° 59′ 45.6″ E 25° 31′ 11″).

The tower dates back to the Hellenic times and is the central part of a fortified farmstead, the kind of which can also be found on other Cyclades islands. The remains of a thick wall surround it almost quadratically. Two chapels crouch next to it. In 2000 an excavation was started, with the objective of restoring and securing the endangered tower, which had been badly damaged by lightning

In the northwest, the wide peak of Zeus towers over the countryside, and a chapel stands closer in the west on a top of a hill.

The famous German archaeologist Ludwig Ross, who travelled intensively through Greece in the 1830s, reported about the tower in his book "Travels on the Islands of the Greek Sea":

"On August 20th , leaving our luggage behind, we rode from Philoti to the so-called Tower on the mountain stream (πύργος τού χειμάρρου) on the southern side of Mount Dia. Three quarters of an hour away from Philoti at the beginning of the mountain rise we saw the marble block which had already been discovered by Tournefort with the inscription Ορος Διος Μηλωσίου. We had to cross over the highest mountain on Náxos, which in its present name (Zia) undeniably retains the island's old name (Δία), near its peak, and from its back, which offered a wide view over many of the islands in the Aegean Sea, even on to Ikaria and Samos, we still had two hours to go to reach the goal of our ride. The tower is an interesting Hellenic ruin, round as a circle, made of white marble square-hewn stones, and still preserved at a height of fifty stone layers or at least as many feet. The entrance is on the southern side. A spiral staircase, formed from the marble projecting from the wall, winds its way up along the inside of the walls. By means of this staircase the defenders could get to the numerous loop-holes. The tower's wall is one meter thick; its inner radius is 7.20 meters. On many of the square stones you can see individual letters, for example, ν, ο, χο, λ, and repeatedly χι. The individual square stone layers are 0.30 to 0.50 meters high. Adjoining the tower there is a square castle courtyard, the walls of which are still partially preserved several feet high and form a 37 meter square.

Nearby Hellenic graves have been found. Was this perhaps a so-called εσχατιά (remote country estate)? The entity is located in the wilderness; this expansive stretch of land south of Mount Dia is almost completely undeveloped. We returned to Philoti along the western side of the mountain in one and a half hours."

If you do not want to take a taxi back to Filóti, you can try to hitch a lift from a passing car. Twelve kilometres on foot to Filóti along the asphalt road can become very strenuous.

The road turns to the southwest in a big arc and passes around the elevation indicated on the map to be 749 m, a mountain spur of the Zeus ridge. On the way up to a pass, you finally reach the **chapel of Ágios Trífon** (5 ¹/₂ hrs/N 37° 0′ 20.3″ E 25° 29′ 3.2 ″), which looks out far over the island.

Two kilometres in the direction of Ágios Trífon at the left-hand

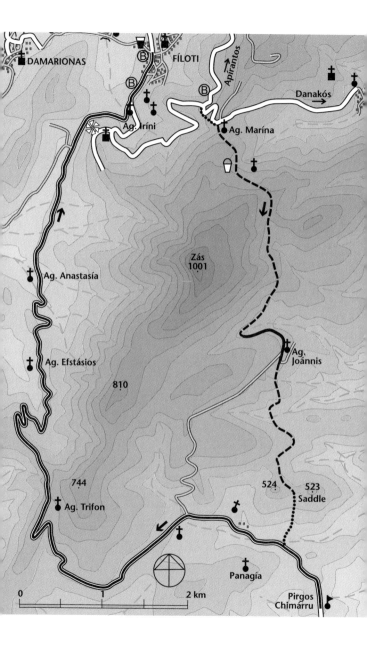

DAMARIONAS

FÍLOTI

Apírantos →

Danakós →

Ag. Iríni

Ag. Marína

Zás
1001

Ag. Anastasía

Ag. Efstásios

Ag. Joánnis

810

744

524
.

523
Saddle

Ag. Trifon

Panagía

Pirgos
Chimárru

0   1   2 km

side of the road is the white-washed **chapel of Ágios Efstásios** (6^1/$_4$ hrs) and after an additional 1.5 kilometres, you also pass, on the left-hand side, the marble-tiled roof **chapel of Agía Anastasía** (page 1) (7^1/$_2$ hrs). The road continues through fields, meadows and olive groves and finally back to **Filóti**, where after a strenuous day you can relax in the tavernas in the village square. The bus stops in front of the tavernas.

⑲ Following Lord Byron's Footsteps?

This approximately four-hour walking tour takes us from the picturesque mountain village of Apíran-tos to an abandoned monastery and further on to Filóti. You will find tavernas and buses at the start and at the end of the tour.

In Apírantos, don't miss visiting one of the four museums (geology, archaeology, folklore and natural history museums). At the beginning of the village you will also find a showroom in which local women exhibit their work, mainly artistic weaving. You should take some time for this attractive village, which was originally settled by refugees from Crete.

rom the main bus stop in **Apírantos** (GPS N 37° 04' 22.0'' E 25° 1' 19.5''), turn south to southwest at the church Kímisis tis Theotókou (Ascension of Mary) into the village. Walk through he village, south to southwest to south, along the small, twist-ng, typical marble-paved alleys, until you reach the asphalt road own the hill.

Walk along this road a while in the direction of Filóti. After a hort time, an asphalt road turns off to the left (¹/₂ hr/N 37° 04' ¹9.0'' E 25° 31' 06.5''); you will possibly find red markings on he surrounding walls. An evergreen oak tree stands at the be-inning. 200 m along this path, in a curve to the left, there is the lain chapel of **Agios Wassilios**. To the east you see a white-vashed double church. The domed church of Ágios Geórgios, esting on the saddle of a hill to the south, points out the direc-ion of this walking tour.

A little way along this wide path you see the natural stone-

coloured chapel of **Agios Pachomios** (³/₄ hr/N 37° 03' 54.0
E 25° 31' 15.6"), crouched low in a meadow to the southeast. Pas
by it on a small path to the south. This chapel is fenced in, bu
one of the naves can be visited.

Follow the small path further to the south until you come to
stream, which is dry in summer. Walk downhill along th
riverbed for 50 m until you come to the junction with a secon
stream. Cross over this stream, heading steeply uphill over fal
en walls directly southwest for about 30 m. Continue walking re
atively steeply uphill to the south. Here there is no visible patl
but instead many animal paths. After a short time **Ágios Geór
gios** can be seen, slightly below the path. Continue through
cluster of large oak trees, keeping the saddle of the hill to th
south in sight.

★ From the **saddle of the hill** (1¹/₄ hrs/N 37° 03' 25.9" E 25° 3
14.0"), you can enjoy the magnificent view back to Apírantos [
and the sea with the islands Makarés and Donoússa ㉗.

Keeping to the left of a wall of wire netting in a southeast direc
tion for 10 minutes, you come to a small **gate** made of steel mes
(1¹/₂ hrs/N 37° 03' 14.5" E 25° 31' 15.8"). From here you will se
the monastery in the south; take the path leading downhill, an
you will reach **Fotodótis** ② (1³/₄ hrs/N 37° 03' 01.5" E 25° 3
17.1") in a few minutes.

> *The fortified, rather deteriorated and long-abandone
> monastery dates back to at least the 15ᵗʰ century. The churcl
> located on the ground floor and freely accessible, is still wel
> preserved. Originally it was probably a basilica with three nave
> over which a dome was later constructed. For many centurie
> visitors have immortalised themselves on the pillars inside. Lor
> Byron allegedly stopped here and found it so beautiful that h
> wanted to die in Náxos.*

Enjoy a pleasant lunch and a fantastic view from a taverna, typ
ical for the area and only open in high-season.

> *Alternative:* A lovely path with steps leads southeast fron
> Fotodótis down to Danakós. If you have enough time, vi
> it this charming remote village. It has several taverna
> Afterwards you can walk up again to the chapel of Agí
> Marina on a beautiful old mule trail.

From the chapel, it is easier to go 100 m west up to a dirt trac
that leads west to the chapel of **Agía Marína** in 30 minutes (2¹/
hrs/N 37° 02' 40.5" E 25° 30' 25.1"). ⑰ ⑱.

From here, take the road to the right and in 10 minutes you wi
reach the main road Filóti-Apírantos (2¹/₂ hrs/N 37° 02' 48.2

25° 30′ 12.8″). Here it is possible to wave down the bus. You
could also walk for 30 minutes along a lovely path with steps to
Filóti and wait for the bus in one of the street cafes. If you choose
this alternative, walk 50 m to the left at the road junction and
then down the steps on the right.

⑳ Ascending Mount Fanári

The four-hour walking tour leads from Apírantos to the peak of Mount Fanári, on down to the vast, fertile high plateau of Tragéa and then to Chalkí. This tour is particularly recommended for people interested in geology. You will be rewarded for your efforts with spectacular panoramic views.

From the main bus stop in **Apírantos** (GPS N 37° 04′ 22.0″ E 2⁵ 31′ 19.5″), walk into the village, passing the church of Kímisis t Theotóku (Ascension of Mary), and turn immediately to th right. Climb up the steps and alleys of this picturesque village the domed church of **Agía Paraskeví** ☐ (also see page 23) (170ε and continue on to the upper edge of the village. A road begir by the remains of a mill. Follow this road uphill for about 100 r to the northwest. At a right-hand turn in the road, a path leac off uphill to the left at a sharp angle, slowly turning to the we (red direction arrows and dots at the junction). After 30 minut you will reach the **flat saddle of a hill** (1 hr/N 37° 04′ 22.5 E 25° 30′ 42.3″), to which you will later return. On the saddle dirt road runs northeast to southwest. Continue a short way t the right along this dirt road until you find, just before a stor wall, the steep path leading up to the peak. On the eastern sic of the Fanári, a stone stairway nestled in the rock makes the f nal climb easier.

On the often windy 883 m high **peak of Fanári** there is the odc looking chapel of Fanariótissa ☐ (1¼ hrs/N 37° 04′ 34.2″ E 2⁵ 30′ 43.9″) with a cistern well. From Fanari, the third highe: mountain on Náxos, you have a wonderful panoramic view. 1 the northwest there is the village of Moní, and from it the fertil high plateau Tragéa stretches out to the south. White spots whic are villages seem to sink into the green of the olive trees. Chalk the destination of our walking tour, lies right in the middle. O a clear day you can see Pírgos Grazia next to the village churc of Protótronos. It is difficult to tell apart Akádimi, next to Chalk from Chalkí. The other villages in the plateau are Kalóxilos, Ke amí. Tsikkalarió, Damariónas and Damalás.

Descend from Fanári, at first going back the way you came to th **flat saddle of the hill**. There go along the dirt road about 30 m until you look down upon a jagged valley (N 37° 4′ 15.8 E 25° 30′ 33.7″). Leave the dirt road here and begin the descer to the right. Usually you can hear the bells of goats and sheep i he distance but can barely see them on the mountain slopes. The hepherd will have seen you long before you notice him. Even in he loneliest of countryside you are never really alone.

specially from this part of the path, you can clearly see the fold-d geological rock formations of the Fanári. (see photo, page 101). When you come to a high stone enclosure, turn to the right. The ath, very visible and marked with red dots, winds downhill in nany serpentine curves. After 300 m, at the timber-line, you

ome to an usually dry stream bed, in which fresh drinking wa-er can be found splashing down from the side in the spring. This s a beautiful place for a rest. From here you can see fertile fields, ended by farmers from Moní. Follow the stream bed to a **fork** 2 hrs/N 37° 04' 26.0" E 25° 30' 17.3"), where red dots and ar-ows point to the right. That is one way to Moní, but you *should ontinue walking in the stream bed* and sometimes along the side f it. Oak and plane trees will give you shade. At some places the vater has worn metre-deep grooves into the marble. The olean-er, which loves dampness, blooms in the late summer. Although teep sections, shrubs, blackberry bushes or fences may hinder our progress at times, it is possible to advance with a little pa-ience and common sense. After descending for 15 to 30 min-tes, you come to a large **cement water-conducting basin** $2^{1}/_{2}$ hrs/N 37° 4' 29.7" E 25° 30' 1.4") on the right side of the tream. From here, a path, shady at first, leads slightly uphill to he left away from the stream. On the left of the path is the chapel **gios Spirídon** ($2^{3}/_{4}$ hrs/N 37° 4' 26.5" E 25° 29' 57.3"). Final-y you come to a dirt path which you follow to the left until you ome to **Kalóxilos** (3 hrs) and, further on, to **Chalkí**. The sched-led bus runs from here. If you still have time, take a rest at the averna Jannis in the village square. It is worthwhile visiting the

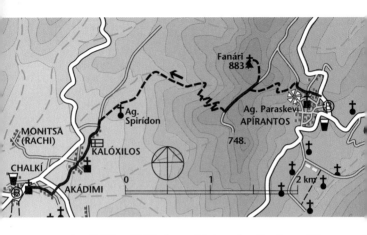

nearby distillery Vallindras, which makes the liquor Kitron, a speciality of Náxos. A few shops can be found here now. Chalkí [is] no longer "a place of the past and very attractive in its decay", as J.T. Bent remarked in 1883.

▷ Below the Platía of **Apírantos** you can find the tavern "Lefteris", where you can sit tranquilly under a walnut tree and enjoy a great view of the valley.

㉑ A Cave with Bats

This walk takes approximately five hours and is some-times without a path. Some climbing is also neces-sary. It brings you first to the peak of the second high-est mountain on Náxos and later to a very solitary, hard-to-find cave. The trail continues to Kóronos.
It is also possible to do a circular walking tour; then it is better to hire a car or scooter and leave it at Stavrós. Tavernas can be found only at the end of the walk. For the mountain peak, a windproof jacket and a flashlight for the cave are recommended.

Take the bus towards Apóllon, through impressive mountai
scenery, and get out at the junction **Stavrós** (GPS N 37° 06' 21.7
E 25° 31' 30.9") near Keramotí. Do not confuse this Stavrós wit
the Tímios Stavrós near Sangrí! Stavrós means in Greek "cross"
From here you have a fantastic view over the east of Náxos.
Start by going uphill to the north along a small, at first somewha
unpretentious dirt path which branches off from the street t
Apóllon diagonally to the left at a sharp angle and runs, at th
beginning, parallel to electric overhead-wires. After a short whil
you reach a dirt road and follow it. Turn left at a fork and ascen
steadily up the south side of the main peak until you reach th
saddle of the peak to the west of the main peak (1¹/₄ hrs/ N 37
07' 35.6" E 25° 31' 01.2"). Here you will find a stone hut su
rounded by a high wall. From here, you can quickly climb th
stony **peak of the Kóronos** (999 m), where you have a panoram
ic view of nearly the whole of Náxos: to the north Apóllon, fa
down to the south Keramotí. To the east, the little islands c
Makarés and Donoússa swim in the sea nearby. The north ridg
of the Kóronos mountain range and also the cave are often wind
and cool and covered in clouds, even when there is fine weath
er below.
At the elevation of the stone hut along the dirt road, walk aroun
the next gentle mountain ridge on the southern side so that yo
can change over to the northern side of the Kóronos range by gc
ing across a ridge to the northwest in front of the second high
est Kóronos peak.
Continue in the same direction, with the peak of the range c
mountains running to the north on your right. Climb steepl
down the northern slope over sharp boulders in a crevice begin

ning here. With a good sense of direction, you will find the 1–1.5 m high entrance of the **Kakó Spílio**, the "bad cave" ② (2 hrs/ N 37° 07' 48.0'' E 25° 30' 15.0''), situated north to northeast. Water runs all year a few metres below the entrance to the cave.

The shepherds tell all sorts of strange stories about this cave and that there was no oxygen in it. An altar is also said to be in the cave. The rear parts of the cave can only be reached by crawling through a very narrow opening, barely as wide as a person. There are bats hanging from the ceiling, as well. ①

The French professor Ernest-Artistide Dugit wrote in 1861:

The Koronis falls off very steeply to the west side also; towards

the north it has many mountain spurs. A valley covered with high forests still existed there in the last century (1). Chestnut trees and green oaks shaded the mastic and strawberry trees. Even stags and wild boars are said to have been there. All of that has disappeared since the war for independence. The only remarkable vegetation still existing today is a fern which is thicker and more lovely than elsewhere on the island. The eastern flank of this mountain has an interesting cave (2): under a kind of covered entry hall there are three rooms which are connected with one another by a flat, narrow passage. The ceiling is as smooth as if it had been chiseled. It can be presumed that this cave could have been one of those primitive places of worship like the Corycian cave on Delphi or that of Trophonius in Livadia, which according to tradition was consecrated to a group of three deities which were usually worshipped in a common cult. At Koronis one could think especially of the three wetnurses of Bacchus, namely the nymphs Koronis, Philia and Cleide. The name Koronis has been preserved through the centuries

and is connected with the mountain, just as the name Jupite
is with Mount Zia (Zeus).

If you want to go to Kóronos, cross over the stream bed in fron
of the cave towards the east. Trodden paths do not exist. From
the opposite sloping ridge, you can not only see the "cave side"
of the Kóronos very well, but also have a wide view out toward
Skepóni in the northwest as far as Engarés in the west. Going
slightly uphill in a southeasterly direction, over cliffs and
through bushes, you come to a few small fields near a stream bec
with plane-trees and a **well**. (2³/4 hrs/N 37° 07' 47.5" E 25° 30
46.6"). Continue to the east, going up a flat saddle directly north
of the main peak (3¹/4 hr/N 37° 07' 47.8" E 25° 31' 10.6") until
you come to a dirt path.

> *Short cut:* If you go along this dirt path to the right, you
> will come to Stavrós.

Continue along the dirt path to the east. By a **sharp fork** in the
path (3¹/2 hrs/N 37° 07' 37.4' E 25° 31' 28.2"), go on to the north
to northest. At a sharp bend, you reach an old monopáti ③ tha
beautifully descends to **Kóronos** (4 ¹/2 hr). There you go along
the asphalt road to the right for about 100 m to the bust o
Nikifóros Mandilarás, who was executed by the military junta ir
1967. From there, the road runs down to the left at a sharp an
gle to the car park. From here you can walk through the winding
alleys to the Information Centre, where you will find useful in
formation about the village and emery mining which used to be
operated in this area.

If you walk on further about 300 m, you will reach the village
square, the Platía. Several small tavernas and kafenía are here
inviting you to rest and relax ④. The bus stops at the statue o
Nikifóros Mandilarás, which you passed earlier.

For those who have left their car at Stavrós, go east through the village at first and then up the steps to the south. Cross the asphalt road and continue, first along an old path with steps on the other side and then on the asphalt road back to **Stavrós**. Here the bus will stop upon request.

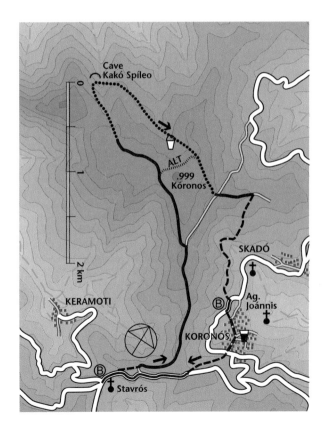

㉒ Frescoes, Emery and Sand

From Apírantos, you walk for about five hours,
first of all to a church with interesting frescoes and
then, passing the remains of an emery mine, to the
beach of Mutsúna. From here you can take a bus
back, but only in the high season. Otherwise a taxi
should be organised. In the high season, several
open tavernas can be found in Mutsúna.

From the main bus stop in **Apírantos** (GPS N 37° 04' 22.0'' E 25°
31' 19.5''), walk under the bridge of the asphalt road and take the
upper, at first very stony and shady, path marked at irregular intervals by red-white signs with "1".

After a little more than a kilometre, you will reach a **wooden sign**
for the closed chapel of Agios Theologes (³/₄ hr/N 37° 04' 49.0''
E 25° 31' 49.0''). Unfortunately, this chapel cannot be viewed, although it contains frescoes from the 13ᵗʰ century.

Do not follow the sign, but instead continue on, following the
path past several gates and crossing an "Alóni", a round, unused
threshing area. In the northeast at the top of a peak, hardly visible, there is a church made of natural stones. This is your next
goal. A wooden sign (Καλλονή Σμυριδορυχεία) points to the last
part of the way to the church **Agía Kiriakí** ① (1¹/₂ hrs/N 37°
05'37.6'' E 25° 32' 36.3'').

> *The church from the 9ᵗʰ century looks plain from the outside,*
> *one could even say plump. However, here are the unique, so-*
> *called an-iconic frescoes ② from the time of the controversy over*
> *image-worship, the Iconoclastic Period in the 9ᵗʰ century. Illus-*
> *trations of gods or saints were often forbidden. Therefore, only*
> *birds and fish in various sizes can be seen in the apse. Circles,*
> *rosettes and crosses are embedded everywhere.*

From the sign mentioned, proceed a little towards the north. The
path winds to the left down into the valley, passing a **spring**
(2 hrs/N 37° 05' 59.5'' E 25° 32' 22.4''). Another sign (Σμυριδορυχεία 20') points the way to the emery area. The path becomes narrow at times as it goes down to a bridge and then on
to some ruins of houses. Emery mineworkers used to live here.
A little further on, you can see the remains of the former **emery mine cable railway** which goes all the way to Mutsúna
(2¹/₂ hrs/N 37° 06' 11.1'' E 25° 32' 44.8''). The cable railway shut
down in 1989 and is now an industrial monument for emery.

mining on Náxos. Full trolleys can still be seen hanging from the cables.

Continue on slightly downhill for 1.5 km along the asphalt road beside the cable railway. Every now and again you can see drilled holes and tunnels in the hillside out of which the emery was mined. Some emery is scattered at on the road (for more details see page 109).

In a 180-degree curve to the right (2³/₄ hrs/N 37° 05′ 54.5″ E 25° 33′ 35.0″), a path leads straight ahead downhill and away from the road, at first steep and then levelling out. After a few minutes you will see, to the east, the peak of the Mutsúna with its characteristic rock. The village of Mutsúna cannot yet be seen. Walk on further, either passing around or going through a **gate** which stands almost in the stream (3 ¹/₂ hrs/N 37° 05′ 29.7″ E 25° 34′ 19.7″) and continue along a dirt road. Cross through a small farm and take the dirt road which first goes southwest to the right and then shortly turns to the left. Follow this path to **Mutsúna** (4 hrs/N 37° 04′ 41.6″ E 25° 35′ 14.8″)

Mutsúna used to be the loading port for emery. ③ A relatively large stockpile and also the loading barges used to transport the emery to the waiting ships still lie around. The village comes alive only in the high season. There are a few tavernas, but they are not open in the low season. Although several holiday homes have been built in the last few years, bus connections are still very poor. If you do not want to take a taxi to return to Apírantos, it takes two to three hours on foot along the road.

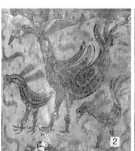

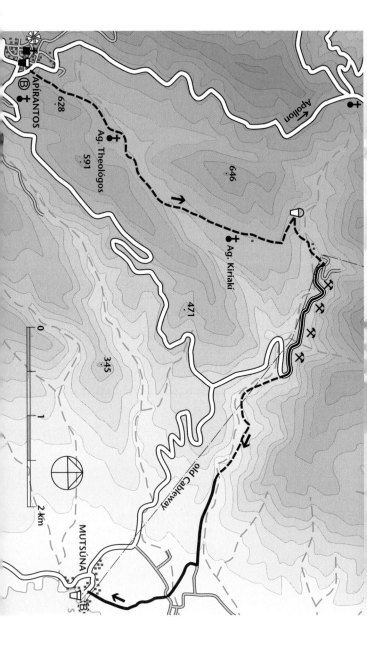

APIRANTOS

628

Ag. Theológos
591

646

Ag. Kiriakí

471

Apollon

345

old Cableway

0

1

2 km

MUTSÚNA

Emery Mining in Náxos

Characteristic of emery are its rusty brown appearance and heaviness. Emery is a mineral mixture of corundum, magnetite, hematite and quartz. Chemically, corundum is an aluminium oxide (Al_2O_3). Its hardness degree of 9 is equal to that of a diamond (10). However, rubies and sapphires, the "noble relations" of corundum, are not found on Náxos. Emery from Náxos is considered to be among the world's finest. It is used as an abrasive, which is why emery boards and sandpaper are made of it. Emery has been mined on Náxos since ancient times, through both open-cast and underground mining. Several of the hills between Kóronos, Apírantos, Liónas and Mutsúna are marked with deep mining shafts. Entering these unsafe mining shafts can be very dangerous.

Emery mining in Náxos reached its commercial peak between the 1920s and the 1960s. In order to ease transport of the mined emery to the port of Mutsúna, a cable railway was built in 1925. 7,000 tons of emery were still being mined in 1978. Some emery is mined even today, but only because it is connected to the emery workers' health and pension insurance. Today natural emery is no longer of any economic importance since synthetic substitutes have taken its place.

In Kóronos there is a visitor centre with information about emery mining in the area. The Emery Museum, which lies a little outside the village, has an exhibition about history and geology and a safe, accessible mining shaft.

㉓ Down to the Pebble Beach

From the "Emery Village" Kóronos, it is a three-hour colourful downhill walk to the unique pebble beach of Liónas. Here there are three tavernas, but they are not all open in the spring.
Return to Kóronos by taxi (Tel.: 228 50-513 89) or possibly by hitchhiking.

Get off the bus at the statue of Nikifóros Mandilarás in **Kóronos** ① (GPS N 37° 07' 08.5'' E 25° 32' 02.8''). This locally born politician was murdered by the military junta in 1967. The road heads downhill to the southeast at a sharp angle to a parking lot. Situated above the local school is a new Information Centre with a large red tiled roof. It is about 100 m from the parking lot and can easily be reached from there through the winding alleys. Here you will find useful facts about the village and emery mining, which has been carried out for a long time.

Continue on downhill to the south through the alleys. After about 300 m you will reach the village square, the Platte (¹/₄ hr/ N 37° 07' 02.4'' E 25° 32' 09.4''), with several small tavernas and kafenía.

From here, start off in a northeast direction to the district Káto Gitoniá (Κάτω Γειτονιά). Walk downhill at the side of the brook and cross it at the first **bridge** (N 37° 07' 03.7'' E 25° 32' 12.4''). In the spring, water still trickles, but the brook is dry in the summer. After about 30 minutes a monopáti forking off to the right leads to the emery-mining region.

★ The route goes downhill north and northwest past the old **arched bridge** (³/₄ hr/N 37° 07' 19.2'' E 25° 32' 34.4'') and comes

to a dirt path. Along it some spectacular views down into the valley can be seen. Follow the path a while, uphill past a barn and then, at a fork in the road, downhill to a wide, **modern bridge** (1 1/2 hrs/N 37° 07' 56.1" E 25° 33' 22.9"). About 250 m after the bridge, the path comes to an end, but a footpath continues. We walk on steeply uphill, particularly at the beginning, accompanied by beautiful views. Several masts from the cable railway of the emery mining region can be seen on the right. The path later nearly always leads downhill and is difficult to find at times. In any case, don't climb too high. After a bit more than 1.5 km, the path reaches a dirt road. At the next fork in the road, proceed on down past the chapel of **Panagía Avdeliótissa** (ΠΑΝΑΓΙΑ ΑΒΔΕΛΙΩΤΗΣΣΑ; 2 1/2 hrs/N 37° 08' 16.0" E 25° 34' 39.5"). The chapel is open, and there is water here all year round.

The dirt road continues for awhile. Pay attention here – in a sharp turn at the end of the road the path leads to the left and is difficult to recognise. The village of Liónas can already be seen from here ②. Descending relatively steeply along the side of a wall, you come to the edge of the village and go down the steps in between the houses to the **beach of Liónas** (3 hrs/N 37° 08' 15.9" E 25° 35' 09.6").

> Liónas is a village with little tourism. There are a number of holiday homes and a few tavernas, but they may not all be open in the low season. At one time emery was shipped from here after being laboriously transported down by mules. In 1925 the transport was moved to Mutsúna due to the cable railway.

The pebble beach of Liónas is unique. After a refreshing swim you can choose your favourite colourful pebble from an enormous variety ③. The return to Kóronos is easiest by taxi. On foot it would take three hours along the asphalt road. The new Emery Mining Museum is on the road just before Kóronos. A walk in an old mine shaft which has been specially prepared for visitors is refreshingly cool, even in mid-summer.

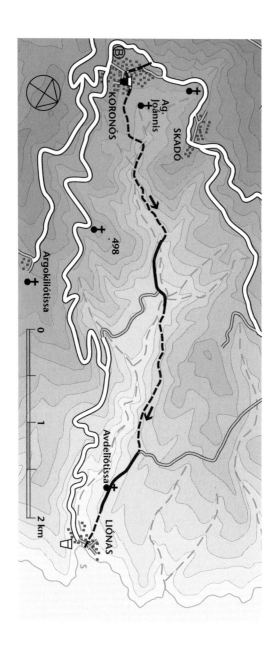

㉔ The Colossus of Apóllon

The walking tour begins after a breathtaking bus ride through the mountains of Náxos. From the 700 m high mountain village of Koronís, it is a pleasant two-hour downhill walk to the most famous youth on Náxos, the giant Kúros. The seaside village of Apóllon has a small beach. Tavernas can be found in Koronís and, above all, in Apóllon.

At the bus stop in **Koronís** (known earlier as **Komiakí**), local wine and cheese can be tasted in the kafeníon at a reasonable price (GPS N 37° 08' 40.8'' E 25° 31' 46.3''). From here, go downhill along the village street. Shortly after the first hairpin bend in the road, a trail noticeably branches off sharply towards the left (N 37° 08' 49.1'' E 25° 32' 01.7''). Follow the red and blue dots which soon appear.

The road to **Apóllon** can be seen on the right as it serpentines down to the sea. Soon the village is also visible, watched over above to the right by the Kalógeros, on the top of which sparse ruins of a Byzantine fort can be found.

After about 2 km, in a sharp curve, you meet up with the **road** again (1 hr/N 37° 09' 51.1'' E 25° 32' 44.3''). Continue slightly uphill to the right of the road for about 200 m and then turn off the road to the left at the next curve (red dots).

At the beginning the path is concrete and later becomes narrow and shaded by trees and bushes. Cross a brook by an old mill and continue slightly uphill. After 200 m to 300 m, you reach the asphalt road again and follow it in the direction of Apóllon. After a short distance the road forks (N 37° 10' 30.4'' E 25° 32' 53.2''), and you should now take the road uphill to the left. After 300 m, the road leads first to the Kúros and then along the northwest shore to the city of Náxos.

*The giant **Kúros** (1 ¹/₂ hrs/N 37° 10' 45,2'' E 25° 32' 53,6'') is an excellent example of Naxian monumental sculpture from the 6th century B.C. Kúroi is the word used for ancient statues of youths.*

The German archaeologist Ludwig Ross was here in 1841:

"After we had climbed over the highest mountain ridge (over 2000 feet high), we came to a wide valley canyon which opened upon Donussa and Amorgos and was full of vineyards, among which the village of Komiaki (η Κωμιακή) is located. After a short rest we climbed down for one and a half hours and came

to the Apollo, a colossal statue still completely in its rough form which is still lying in the quarry in which it was carved, 10 minutes from the riverbank on the slope of an average-sized hill made completely of white marble. Meanwhile it had become evening, and we had to bivouac outdoors here. We had our beds laid out on the statue itself."

The figure stands and was intended to be naked. It is recognised by archaeologists to resemble the same form and position as the *Apóllon Patroos* or *Pythios*: the left foot protruding, similar to the debris of the Naxian colossus of *Délos*; both arms resting on the sides from the elbows upwards resting and half-raised from the elbows downwards, stretching outwards across the chest, like the Philistine *Apóllon of Kanachos*. The exact dimensions are: overall height of the figure from the foot-sole to the top of the head 10.60 meters (ca.34 feet); chest width 1.70 metres; length of the upper arms from shoulder to elbow 1.90 meters. The eyes are indicated by two hollows and the nose by an elevation.

Five minutes away from this statue, on the same marble hill, an inscription on a smooth wall states in beautiful three-inch letters: ὅρος χωρίου ιερου Απόλλωνος. This inscription probably contributed to keeping the name of the colossus alive today amongst the locals, who still call him: τον Απόλλωνα. This name cannot have been learnt from travellers; Tournefort, who was not aware of the existence of the statue, found the name already in use and took it to name the small anchorage on this side of the island. According to him, it is certain that no other travellers came here except for Pasch van Krienen. Moreover, it appears that Bondelmonte also spoke about this figure, although rather confusedly and unclearly.

"What was the purpose of the colossus originally? It could be possible that it was destined to remain on the island since, in addition to the inscription already mentioned, other pieces of evidence verify sufficiently an Apollo cult on *Náxos*. A shrine

O P O Σ
X Ω P I O Y
I E P O Y
A Π O Λ Λ Ω N O Σ

1

to the Delian deity was located near the city. According to other information Apollo was worshipped as Tragios or Tragia or Tragea, which may be a city on Naxos or even more likely, as I believe, the little island known nowadays as Makares between Náxos and Donussa. It is probable, however, the incompleted colossus was originally intended as a votive offering on Delos since its measurements correspond quite closely to those of the remains of the statue there. In that case the completion of the colossus would have been given up due to several fairly deep cracks which run diagonally across the face and over the chest, and another better marble block would have been chosen in its place. To that I must make the observation that the white marble, of which almost half of Náxos consists, is of almost the same stone and quality as that of Paros, although it is not as famous."

Alternative: If you walk uphill in the direction of the longitudinal axis of the statue for about 10 minutes, through quite thorny bushes to the other side of the hill, you will find, carved in a steep wall, an ancient inscription meaning something like: Boundary of the sacred region of Apóllon. (N 37º 10' 39.1'' E 25º 32' 51.0''). The letters, taken from the photograph, can be seen at the right of the illustration ①.

From the Kúros, walk to the left along the road for about 50 m and then to the right along small paths. In a few minutes you will reach the village of **Apóllon**, where you can catch the bus for the return trip. There is a small sandy beach where you can take a refreshing swim and taste Greek fast-food at one of the many tavernas.

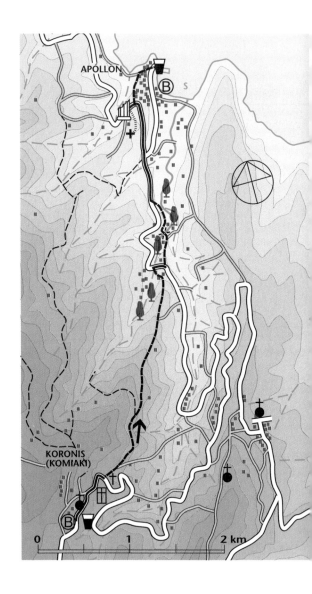

㉕ Water and Wine

After passing a big new reservoir and walking through a wine growing region, you end this tour at a very special taverna after about six hours. Part of this walk goes through partly unmarked, rough open country. Therefore, you should familiarise yourself well beforehand. It is best to take a taxi there and back. Otherwise, enquire when a bus from Apóllon passes Abrám in the afternoon so that you can wave it down there. It is also possible to spend the night at the end of the walk.

The **Monastery of Faneroménis** is located at the side of the road along the west coast.

The massive, almost windowless and fortress-like monastery dates from the 17th century. It has been renovated and shines brightly in dazzling white. It is inhabited by a few monks. The entrance to the courtyard and to the chapel of the monastery is guarded like a castle. It is not possible to see more than the exterior.

The walking tour begins towards the east on a dirt road to Skepóni which forks off the asphalt road to the right (GPS N 37° 08' 25.4" E 25° 27' 43.1") and leads uphill along a wide dirt road to the largest **reservoir** on the island. A dam was completed in 2003 with the financial support of the European Union. This reservoir is supposed to ensure the water supply for the island throughout the entire year. It is meant mainly for irrigation purposes and only partly for domestic use. With an area of 100 m x 260 m and a depth of up to 30 m, the reservoir can hold 1.5 million cubic metres of water.

After about two kilometres, you pass a small farm and come to a fork in the path, where you take the path down to the left and then cross a brook. Soon you will see several houses on top of the protruding rocks – Skepóni, a mountain village only inhabited in the summer. Several farmers have fields here. Just before **Skepóni**, leave the dirt road, cross another riverbed and climb up steeply to the houses (1 hr/N 37° 08' 32.4" E 25° 29' 39.2").

From Skepóni, ascend relatively steeply to the northeast in or to the right of the dry riverbed. The goal is a relatively flat pass 300 m above sea level. No path is recognisable, but the presence of a few trees makes the going easy here. Somewhat later, shrubs, blackberry bushes and fences make it more difficult.

Many dirt roads cross the **pass** (2 hrs/N 37° 09′ 0.5″ E 25° 30′ 8.3″). One leads to the east towards Mirísis and Komiakí. On a clear day Ktapódia, the small uninhabited neighbouring island of Mýkonos, can be seen to the north. The cliffs on the opposite side are stony and barren. The few houses of Mirísis, our half-way goal are down below, about 150 m to the northeast. The white chapel of Agía Anastasía is to the left.

From the pass, proceed to the north, crossing a fence and climbing down to Mirísis quite directly and steeply. Mýkonos can also been seen from here now. Further down, just before Mirísis, it becomes difficult to cross the riverbed and the field. The local farmers know better paths, but unfamiliar hikers need patience and feeling. When you come to the village of **Mirísis**, turn to the left on a dirt road to the chapel of Agía Anastasía. ① (3 hrs/N 37° 09′ 24.8″ E 25° 30′ 26.2″). Thanks to the water from the river all year round, this has always been a good area for agriculture, above all for wine.

You can see the dirt road leading to the sea in serpentine curves. Take a short cut directly from the chapel along a path going downhill to the northwest. After 30 m, the path turns to the right at a place marked by two old telephone poles. You come to a small dead-end path leading back to the dirt road. Continue to the left and cross the **riverbed** (3¹/₂ hrs/N 37° 09′ 42.9″ E 25° 30′ 10.7″). After a while you will see, to the northwest, the goal of our walking tour, the small beach of Abrám with several houses. Half an hour later you come to the asphalt coastal road of Náxos (4 hrs/ N 37° 10′ 2.9″ E 25° 29′ 3.5″), where you swing to the right. About 150 m to the left is the turnoff to **Abrám**. After 600m you will see the taverna "Efthímios". From May to October you can en-

joy the sea view from the terrace and taste the good, simple dishes and the home-made wine while watching the sun set ②, with the unique sculptures of the sculptor Rókkos in the foreground. Rental rooms are available (tel. 228 50-632 44), or you can call a taxi. A dip on the pebble beach beforehand might be a good idea. If you happen to see it in time, you can wave down the bus on the road above to the right.

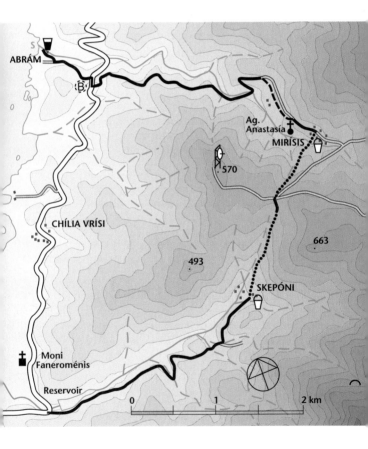

㉖ Walking along the Riverside

From the mountain village of Kinídaros, this walk takes four hours down through a fertile valley and along the most water-abundant river on Náxos to Engarés. From there you can arrange for a taxi to collect you at one of the tavernas.

From the bus stop in **Kinídaros** (War Memorial; GPS N 37° 06' 04.3" E 25° 28' 45.6"), *do not* follow the sign pointing to Agios Artémios, but instead walk upwards for nearly a kilometre over steps and along alleys through the picturesque village situated on the slope. At the top, on a dirt road to the north, you reach a flat pass (¹/₄ hr/N 37° 06' 24.8" E 25° 28' 41.4"). After a while you should pass a marble quarry on the right-hand side (otherwise, you have walked too far east). Some time after crossing the pass, you will recognise the three-nave basilica of Ágios Artémios, an unusual structure on the Cyclades, surrounded by cypresses down in a fertile valley to the north. The green of the valley stands out strongly against the barren, stony cliffs overhead. Far to the north is Engarés, the goal of the walking tour.

The dirt road twists down into the valley in steep serpentine curves for several hundred metres, leads over a bridge and then forks. This dirt road can be followed to Ágios Artémios, but it is rather boring. With a good sense of direction, you should be able find a greater part of the original monopáti. Red lines and blue dots help, and the dirt road is partly incorporated into this route. Several hundred metres *before* a bridge, there is a not too noticeable **junction** (³/₄ hr/N 37° 06' 47.0" E 25° 28' 26.2"), marked by a blue arrow on a stone, that turns to the right and goes directly down to the valley.

After about 300 m, you reach the river (1 hr/N 37° 06' 52.0" E 25° 28' 29.2"). The city of Náxos obtains its water from the springs up above.

★ There are crabs, eels and frogs here. If you approach carefully, you can even see turtles, which have survived only because they are inedible. Cross the river, balancing on stones or barefoot, and then go directly to the **basilica of Ágios Artémios** ① (1¼ hrs N 37° 06' 56.1" E 25° 28' 32.7"). If you happen to miss the path, the 300 m to the church can be managed without it.

> *Ágios Artémios, in its present form, dates from the 18th century. It is the largest church outside the city of Náxos. Unfortunately, it is now nearly always closed. A hundred metres away are the ruins of the chapel of Ágios Dimítrios, which once probably had a monastery.*

To return, first go back the same way, i.e., across the river and uphill to a fork in the path marked with blue arrows and red dots. From here, a small path leads downhill to the right. After about 300 m, you reach the road and the river again at a **two-arched bridge** (1¾ hrs/N 37° 06' 44.0" E 25° 28' 02.3").

From the bridge, do not go along the dirt road but instead along the north side and under the bridge to the river. Then work your way along the north side of the river, occasionally nearly in the river. Sometimes wet feet are unavoidable. Markings will help you to find the way. Eventually you will reach two small cement **overflow weirs** (2¼ hrs/N 37° 06' 38.7" E 25° 27' 55.1") not far apart from each other. At the second one, which is about 1.5 m wide, cross the river. On the south side, past a small dilapidated stone hut, an inconspicuous path begins from the river and leads uphill to the southwest.

In the spring, a cascade-like **waterfall** ②, whose water comes from Kinídaros, can be seen on the left. This is a unique spectacle in the dry Cyclades.

The small path leads westwards along the slope, about 50 to 100 m above the river. In the spring, it can be quite wet and muddy; thorny bushes often make the going difficult. The path eventually leads to a dirt road that connects the surrounding fields. It would be easy to go back to Engarés along this dirt road, but the loveliest way is to take the old path past the chapel of **Ágios Geórgios** (2¾ hrs/N 37° 06' 44.5" E 25° 27' 02.9"). After passing the chapel, continue on down to the river, where the path makes a sharp bend to the right. Blackberry bushes sometimes make the going difficult. Markers will help you find the way. It follows a dilapidated **aqueduct**, whose water flows to an old mill. Due to

he abundance of water there are many orchards here.
he path **crosses the river** (3 hrs/N 37° 06' 47.3'' E 25° 27' 02.2'')
and leads along and sometimes in the river bed. At many places
n the water there are very shy turtles  that plop into the water
at the slightest noise. If you wait quietly for a while, they surface
after a few minutes to carry on basking in the sun. The path,
marked with dots, leads back over the river then northeast away
from the river and uphill along the slope. After walking in a long
semicircle you will eventually reach the uninhabited **Pírgos
Brandúna**, situated below the path (3 1/4 hrs/N 37° 06' 53.1''
E 25° 26' 39.5''). The family coat of arms (Bild 4) with the inscription: ANDRONIKOS PRADOUNAS is above the entrance.
From here you will see something white-washed on a conical-
shaped hill to the north, just below the peak. This is Jénnissis,
one of the many small cave chapels of Náxos. According to a
myth, Diónysos was said to have been born here.
At the pírgos you can see the first houses of the village of **Engarés**
(Mitriá). After a further kilometre you will reach the centre of the
village, where you can take some refreshment and then order a
taxi. In the high season the bus goes past here.

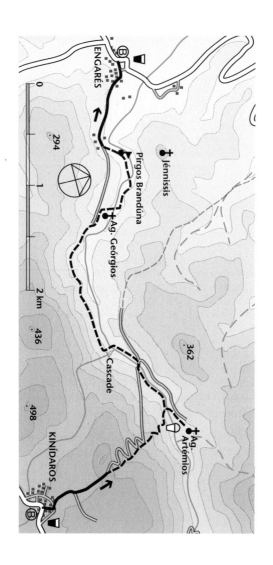

Erimonísia
Small Cyclades
Kleine Kykladen

Between Náxos and Amorgós there are a few small islands just waiting for visitors who think back with regret to the time when tourism was just beginning. The translation of the name of these islands, the "Forsaken Islands" – also called "Erimonísia" or "Nisides" – comes from the time when they were uninhabited. The residents had abandoned the islands for several centuries since pirates used the bays as a hide-out, and they didn't return until after the Greek war for independence.

The group of islands consists of six larger and twenty smaller islands, but only four are inhabited. One of these is the island of Koufoníssia, which is now well-visited – especially in August. The other islands are still very natural, which comes from the fact that the big ferries don't anchor here very often.

It is easy to get here from Náxos: on board the "Skopelitis", a newer, somewhat trim ship, which has meanwhile replaced its legendary predecessor after many years of good service.

In season it provides daily service from the side pier in Náxos. However, passengers without "sea legs" can have their problems during a rough crossing.

Anyone who doesn't need a menu but instead still wants to choose his meal in the kitchen and would like to see the guests from the evening before in the few simple tavernas again the next evening should sail over here on board the "Skopelitis" for a few pleasant days.

Donoússa

The most northerly and remote of the "Small Cyclades" is very mountainous and practically treeless. Geologically, it is composed of marble, quartzite and schist. Sometimes it is possible to buy a simple map of the island in the harbour taverna. Unfortunately, a road has largely destroyed the former mule track leading around the island. The route described here runs along parallel paths, thus making an attractive tour of the island possible again.

㉗ Tour of the Island

The five to six-hour trek begins with an innocuous climb to about 250 m and a descent to the wide bay of Kalotarítissa. After a short climb, a horizontal route around the island is taken. There are cisterns on the way – but no tavernas. The distance is approximately 10 km.

Depart from below the **village church** of Timios Stavros, heading northwards. Past the schools you reach a lane, cross the track, leaving the "windmill" behind you on the left, and climb slowly up a mule track to the left of a dry bed. After crossing the mule track, the path climbs gently until you reach a windy **pass** (1 hr) below Mt. Papás. Looking down over the protected bay ①, along past the cliffs, turn down to the left to the unspoilt hamlet of **Kalotarítissa** (1 ¹/₂ hrs). From there, head on along a monopáti whose days are very probably numbered – it is intended that tourism should also come to Kalotarítissa. For the present, however, it still leads you leisurely along the coast and then uphill – until you meet the unsealed road. An eight-metre wide monstrosity has been carved into the landscape. Absurd for the handful of cars there are on the island at present. The road has been built for a holiday colony planned down near the bay.

The old monopáti lies buried under it. Only later, in a right-hand curve, when a fence comes into view down below to the left, can one flee from this monstrosity and reach **Mersíni** (2 ³/₄ hrs) without a path by going left across the terraces.

Short cut: By taking the road, you will rejoin the trail before Messaría. Time saved: 30 min.

After taking the steep concrete path downhill in Mersíni, you see a round, rusty German naval mine on the right, leaning peacefully against the wall of a courtyard in the sun, and the you arrive at a **spring** (3 hrs) ② five minutes later. The water splashes wondrously beneath the huge acorn tree throughout the year ("drinking water, no washing, no nudism").

Turning back a few metres, you now head left above the (EU) solar collectors until you meet a path leading down left. Keeping to the right, you arrive at the often deserted sandy bay of **Livádi** (3 ½ hrs) and feel like Robinson Crusoe. There are tamarisks and some spring water.

On the opposite side, at the stone cairn, continue uphill along a trail and then, higher up, without a path to the round **stump of a windmill** (4 hrs). If you trudge on inland going downhill from here, you will soon find a monopáti leading to the wide dirt road. Take the left bend of the road at the cleft in the valley (water culvert), taking care not to overlook the narrow way heading up on

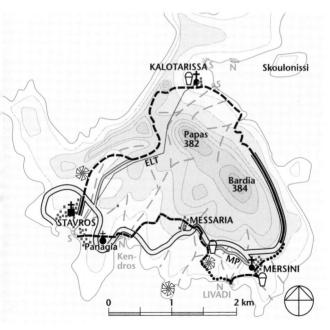

the right after 50 m. This takes you to the upper part of the hamlet of **Messaría** (4 ¹/₄ hrs) and, at the next right fork, straight on and then down into the valley. Here, cross the dirt road and follow the dry bed towards Kéntros beach for 50 m before taking what is left of the old path up on the right. Proceed another 80 m along the road and then after the electricity cables up to the right to the double church of Panagía, and, from there, down to **Stavros** (5 hrs).

Iráklia

You still find the charm of earlier Cycladic sojourns on this mountainous island. It is well suited for hiking as some of the old mule tracks have survived and are still in use. A pretty good map of the island can be bought from the taverna near the harbour.

㉘ The Cave of St. John

This five-hour trek leads to the famous cave of St. John below Mt. Papás, the highest mountain on the island. The return journey takes you via Panagía, in reality the main village of the island. One can't necessarily rely on the tavernas being open here in the low season. When visiting the cave you should take a torch or candles or, at least, a lighter with you.

Leave the village starting from the **Taxiarchis Church** at the top end of the village along a roadway.
At the second **fork** (¹/₄ hr) bear *right* onto a narrow path which soon becomes a trail. You are guided by a wall to the left, soon joined by another on the right: the monopáti is now whole again and you can turn your attention back to the view. Below the hamlet continue straight ahead and, just before it, after the gate, climb the last few metres on the old monopáti up to **Ágios Athanássis** (1 hr).
Having walked through the group of three modest houses, you reach a gate after the third house and then another monopáti leading to a ditch. On the other side go uphill following the route markings and keeping slightly to the left. At the top of the **ridge** (1¹/₂ hrs) go through an opening in the wall. Head on downhill for a while without a trail until you see a clear path above the bay ★ leading around the mountain. It leads directly to the **cave of Ágios Ioánnis** (2¹/₄ hrs). ☐

On the left is the large cave chamber where the big church festival takes place on August 29, for which the entire population of the island gathers. On the right is a small cave with a bell in front of it. If you light a few of the candles around the altar inside, you can perhaps imagine the atmosphere

during the festivities. The other chambers cannot be explored alone.

Return the same way, climbing back up to the **ridge** (2³/₄ hrs).
Alternative: Of course, the real mountain enthusiast will quickly ascend the 100 metres up to the **summit of Mt. Papás** (419 m) in 20 min., take a quick look over to Santoríni, contentedly passing the chapel of Profitis Elias on the way to Panagía (overall length: one hour).

The more relaxed hikers will take the trails leading down from the pass and, at the ditch, a monopáti to **Panagía** (3¹/₄ hrs).  Here, below the church, you find "To Steki" – an all-in-one general store-bakery-kafeníon. Sometimes another kafeníon is open further on down.

Turn down to the left two houses below "To Steki" onto a mule track. After the ditch at the end of the path there is a **field altar** (3 ¹/₂ hrs). Proceed 30 m uphill, over a wall and along a rather crumbling monopáti. Having passed around the walled vineyard on the right and climbed over another wall, you meet the **way up** (3 ³/₄ hrs) again, continue on down and turn left at the fork towards the village of **Ágios Geórgios**.

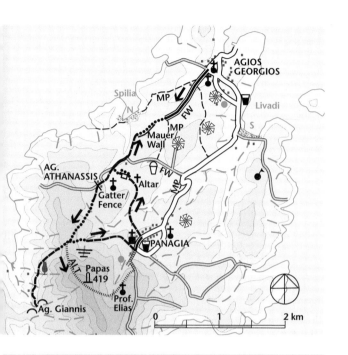

Island Hopping

It is no problem to reach other islands from Náxos. The most pleasant way is on the big ferries, with a lot of room on the upper deck and comfortable, but often smoky, lounges, restaurants and cabins on the lower decks. The main route for the ferries runs between Piräus, Páros, Náxos and Santoríni, with several crossings daily. Sámos and Rhódos can also be reached easily from Náxos.

In addition, there are numerous other cross-connections with fast, smaller ships and katamarans. These are, however, much more expensive.

In the main season the MS "Skopelitis" has daily connections from Náxos to the Small Cyclades. From there, there are further ship connections to Amorgós.

Koufoníssia

Most visitors are attracted by the long sandy beaches. That is why the very small, flat island of Epáno Koufoníssia with its sparse vegetation can become overcrowded in August. There are few houses and no chapels outside the village as the island was only repopulated 200 years ago.

㉙ Beachcombers

This practically level 12-kilometre route along the west coast with its multicoloured rock formations leads to the wide sandy bay of Porí, then past several other sandy beaches back to the village. There is a beach taverna near the end of the tour.

From **St. George's Church**, head west on the road running through the village, turning right at each of the two forks and continuing down to the bay with the island's shipyard ①. Captain Nikolas' fish taverna and an ouzerie fill up here in the evenings. You soon reach the protected fishing port along the dirt road. Behind it looms Náxos, huge in comparison with this tiny island.

> *Short cut:* After the **wall** (¹/₄ hr) in the middle of the harbour boundary, turn right into a field, cross it and, when you come to a path further on, take the left fork uphill. At the stone house above, continue without a path, past shady picnic spots, to the only hill on the island and then down from here into the **hollow** (30 min.).

On the northern **side of the harbour** (¹/₄ hr), a field path leads along the brightly coloured rocky coastline and then continues without a path until, 30 min. outside the harbour, the way leads up along a dry bed to the refuse dump. Take the access road leading to a **hollow** (1¹/₄ hrs). Here a footpath branches off to the left (red dots), at the end of which you climb over a wall, continuing first to the right along a field and then across country to reach the long sandy beach of **Porí** (1³/₄ hr). To the left of it are bizarre cliffs ②. This is a good place to rest – provided you have brought along something to drink.

Short cut: A monopáti leads directly from the end of the beach onto a roadway to the village.

There is a wide trail leading along the coast, past beautiful sandy beaches, to the hotel complex of **Finikas** (2½ hr). Here you can fortify yourself for the last stage of the tour to **Chóra** (3 hr) at the shady beach taverna.

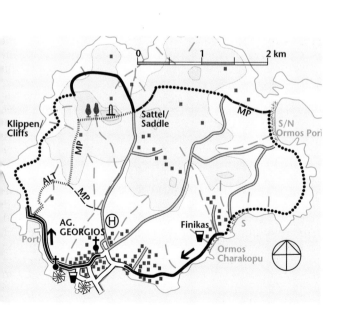

Schinoússa

Both from the map and from the sea, this member of the "Small Cyclades" appears more rugged than it is in reality. A closer look reveals gently rolling hills, meadows and even pasture land, large cisterns, small olive groves, vineyards and noticeably few chapels. The topography has always permitted the use of horse-drawn vehicles, which has led to the fact that there are relatively few mule tracks.

㉚ Three Sandy Coves

The longest beaches are found in the south below Chóra; you will visit three other small, isolated coves. There are no tavernas or serviceable cisterns on the trek. Three to four hours are needed to complete this circular route with very few inclines, though several waist-high field walls do have to be surmounted.

You begin on the north side of the village at the **bakery**, heading away from the houses, and turn downhill to the right after 80 m into the lovely countryside, with numerous islands and islets floating in the sea beyond ①. After a cistern (right), go through a wide **gate** (¹/₄ hr), bear left past the next cistern on the right and wander above a stony bay before continuing along the coast, either without a path or along trails, and around the hill

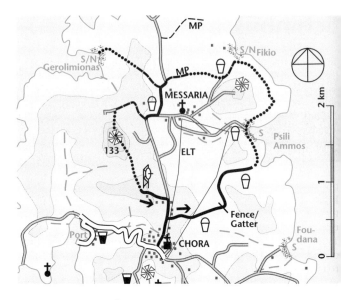

to the **bay of Psilí-Ámmos** (³/₄ hr). It is forbidden to anchor here as the electricity ring main, which now links the islands with Náxos, runs along the sea floor. Thanks to this, the noisy diesel generators of earlier days have now become superfluous.

You head on over easily recognisable trails along the rocky coastline. Wide terraces allow a broader view up to the highest mountain of the Cyclades, Mt. Zeus (1001 m) on Náxos. The next sandy beach, **Fikío Beach** (1¹/₄ hrs), is more to our liking!

The way heads inland at some ruins, passing to the left of the vineyard and left at the end of a wall onto a mule track. After a few metres, you have to climb over a stone wall on the right and then walk along the edge of the fields towards the windmill. Having jumped nimbly over another two walls, you come to a mule track leading to an unsealed road. Follow this to the left for 50 m before **turning off** (1¹/₂ hrs) to the right. Fairly soon the path stops in a dead end and you continue on down without a trail to the small **sandy cove** (2 hr). Well, wasn't it worth it? If you're lucky, you will have the 21 metres of sand alone to yourself.

You return by going back up to the roadway, turning right, then right again up an incline from the cistern. At the left bend you take the flagstone path to the right, and later head up left with-

out a trail though the field to the **windmill** ($2^3/_4$ hr). This is the highest point on the island; inside the well-preserved mill, the technically interested will wonder why the millstones are so high up.

The village is reached by proceeding through the hollow without a trail, the antenna to your left, and then on downhill to the road to **Schinoússa**.

> ▷ At the hotel "Anesis" you can purchase a decent map of the island (and enjoy a fantastic night view from one of the rooms over to Santoríni, starry sky included).

Some Greek for hikers

jássas	hello	ikonostasio	altar screen
ne/óchi	yes/no	chóra	main village
parakaló	please	chorió	village, hamlet
efcharistó	thank you	spíti	house
endáxi	okay	platía	square
sto kaló	all the best	paralía	harbour
posin óra ?	how long ?		promenade
pósso makriá	how far is	kástro	Venetian castle
ine ja	it to ...	pírgos	Venetian
puíne	where is ...?		fortified tower
óra	hour	langádi	gorge, ravine
neró	water	xirolithía	dry-stone wall
psomí	bread		
tirí	cheese	wounó	mountain
isía	straight ahead	thálassa	sea
dexiá	right	pigí	fountain,
aristerá	left		spring
apáno	up, upwards	órmos	bay
káto	downwards	meltémi	strong nor-
leoforió	bus		therly wind
stásis	bus stop	drómos	street
papás	Greek priest	odós	street
eklisiá	church	skála	stairway
moní,	monastery	monopáti	donkey trail
monastíri		odiporó	walking
ksoklísi	rural chapel	phrígana	scrub, the
panagía	Mother of God		enemy of the
panigíri	parish fair		island hiker
ágios, agía, AG	saint ..		

Useful Phone numbers

Phone numbers on Náxos (area code 22850):
Taxis Chóra 22444, Filóti 31328 and 75282
Police / Tourist police 22100

Abbreviations, Key

———	hiking route on a road or dirt track
– – – –	hiking route on a path
••••••••••	hiking route without a path
⸱⸱⸱⸱ALT⸱⸱⸱⸱	alternative route/short cut
ST	road
FW	unclassified road/dirt track
_ _MP_ _	monopáti/mule track
— — —	dry streambed (at times) / hollow
← ⇐	direction of route
⚑	antennae
♪ ♪	Venetian fortress/dwelling tower, ruins
Ⓑ ⦂Ḃ⦂	bus stop/at times
⊞	cemetery
⌒	cave
Ⓗ	helicopter landing pad
⬢ ▫	houses, ruins
✝	monastery/large church
✝ ✝ ♪	chapel, summit church, ruin
⛪	ancient ruins/statues
s	beach
Ⓣ	petrol station
▼ ▽	tavern, open seasonally
Ⓟ	car park
❋	windmill/ruins
⬂ ▫	cistern/well/spring
★	The authors' 10 favourite spots

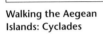

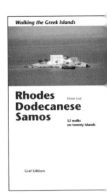

Walking the Aegean Islands: Cyclades

ISBN 3-9803130-5-0
2004:
ISBN 3-9808802-1-4

Wandern auf den Kykladen

ISBN 3-9803130-4-2
ab 2004:
ISBN 3-9808802-0-6

Rhodes, Dodecanese, Samos

ISBN 3-9803130-9-3
published 2004

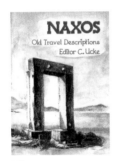

**Náxos
Old Travel Descriptions**
ISBN 3-923666-6-3

**Náxos
Alte Reisebeschreibungen**
ISBN 3-3-923666-10-1

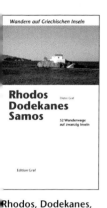

Walking the Greek Islands
Wandern auf Griechischen Inseln

Rhodos, Dodekanes, Samos

ISBN 3-9803130-8-5
erscheint 2004

We would be very grateful for information
about changes in paths and similar data
and as a token of our appreciation we will
send you a free copy of our next edition.
Up-dates can be found under the followin
Internet sites.

Graf Editions
Elisabethstr. 29
D-80796 Muenchen
Germany
Tel. 0049-89-2715957
Fax 0049-89-2715997
www.graf-editions.de

Christian Ucke
www.ucke.de
Complete GPS routes can be found here.

©2003 Edition Dieter Graf, Munich
All rights reserved.
Original title: „Naxos und Kleine Kykladen"

Layout: Hol Triooh
Maps: Kurt Zucher, Starnberg
Translation: Nancy Kuehler, Linda Andrews

ISBN 3-9803130-7-7